SOCK MONKEYS
HAVE ISSUES

GREG STONES

CHRONICLE BOOKS

SAN FRANCISCO

Huge thanks to Brooke for tolerating this crazy pipe dream of
mine, Tom and Gabriele for making me go to college, Steve
Mockus from pulling me away from my darker tendencies,
and Michael Morris for making my books look awesome!

Library of Congress Cataloging-in-Publication Data available.

ISBN 978-1-4521-4005-6

Manufactured in China

MIX
Paper from
responsible sources
FSC® C008047

FSC
www.fsc.org

Designed by Michael Morris

10 9 8 7 6 5 4 3 2 1

Chronicle Books LLC
680 Second Street
San Francisco, California 94107
www.chroniclebooks.com

Chronicle Books publishes distinctive books and gifts. From
award-winning children's titles, bestselling cookbooks, and
eclectic pop culture to acclaimed works of art and design,
stationery, andjournals, we craft publishing that's instantly
recognizable for its spirit and creativity. Enjoy our publishing and
become part of our community at www.chroniclebooks.com.

SOCK MONKEYS HAVE ISSUES WITH . . .

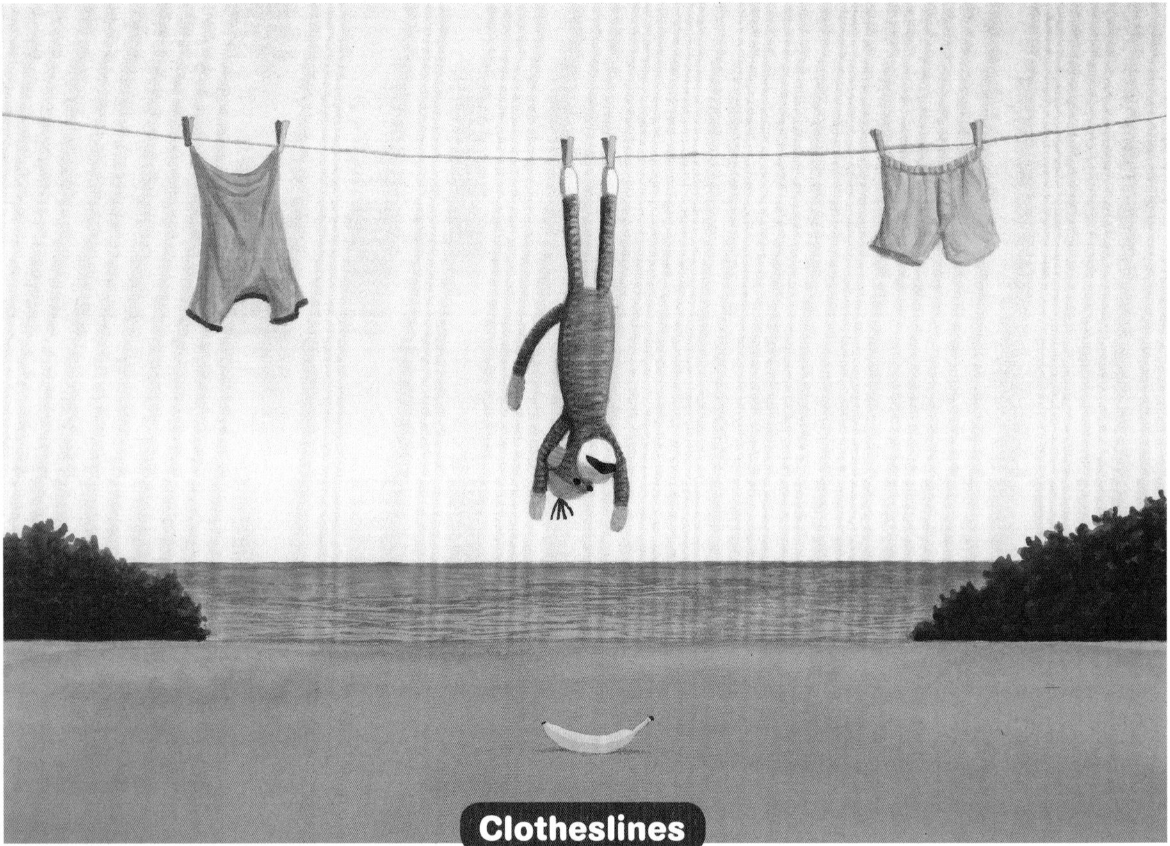

Clotheslines

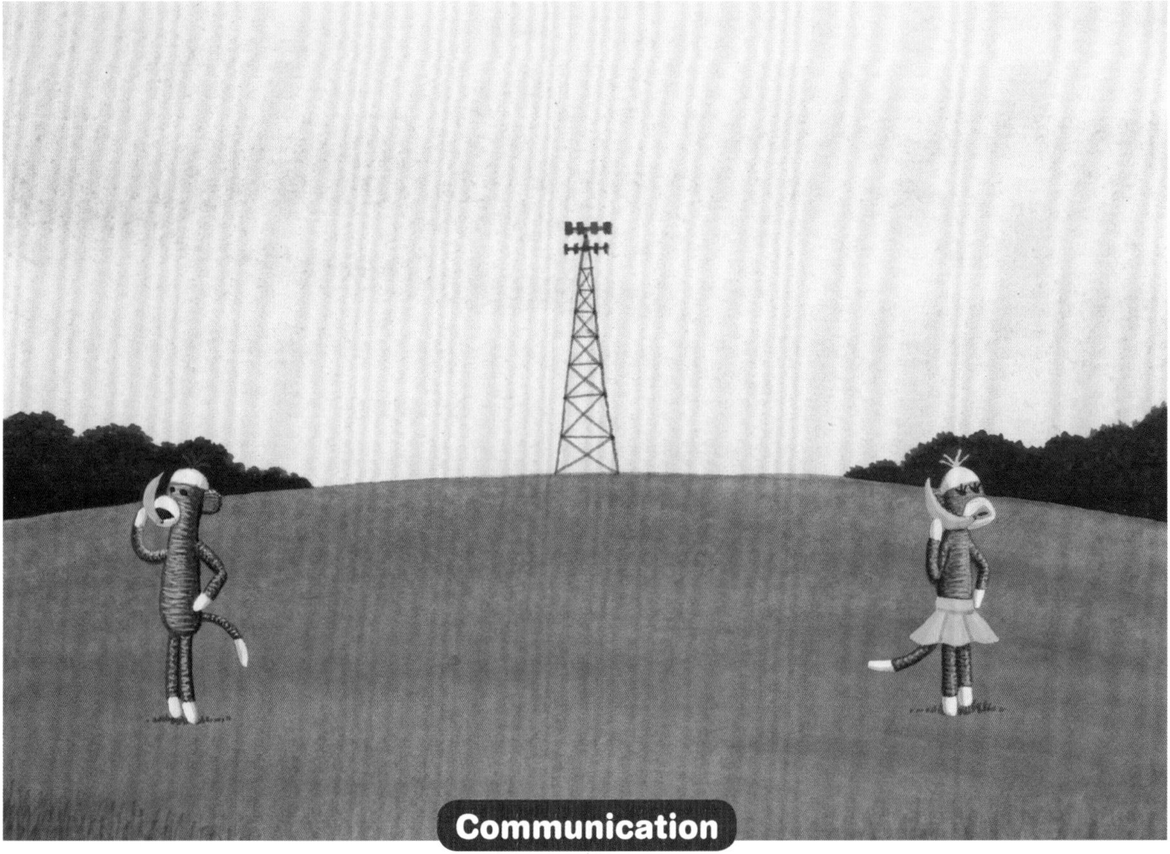
Communication

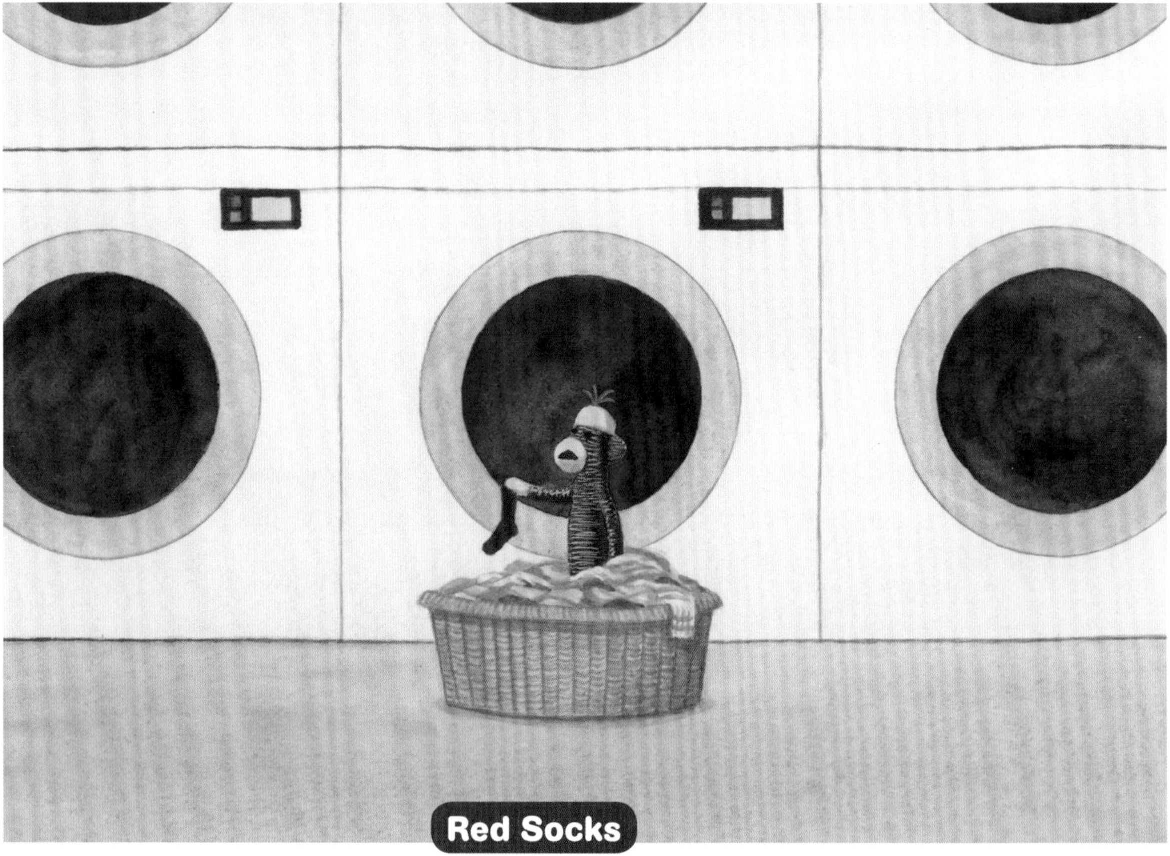
Red Socks

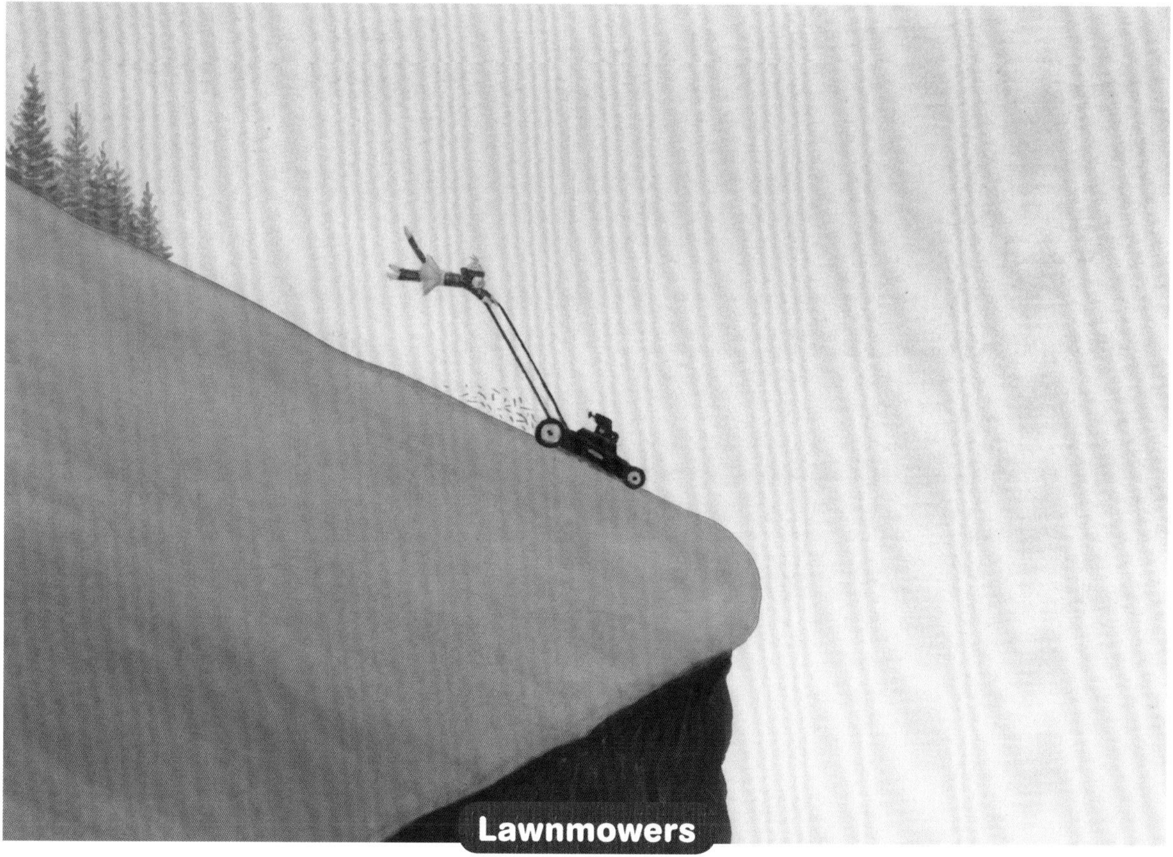

Lawnmowers

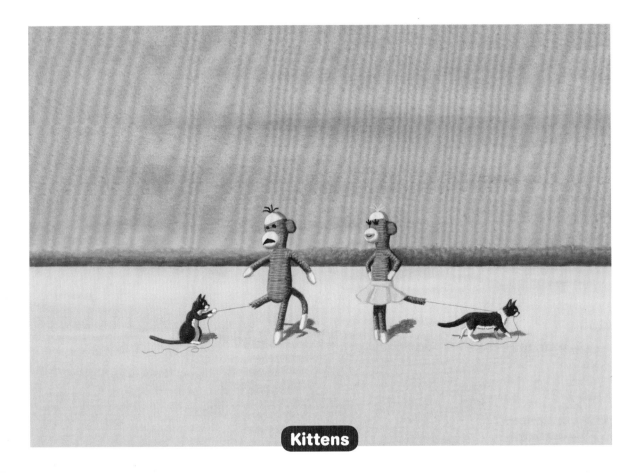

Kittens

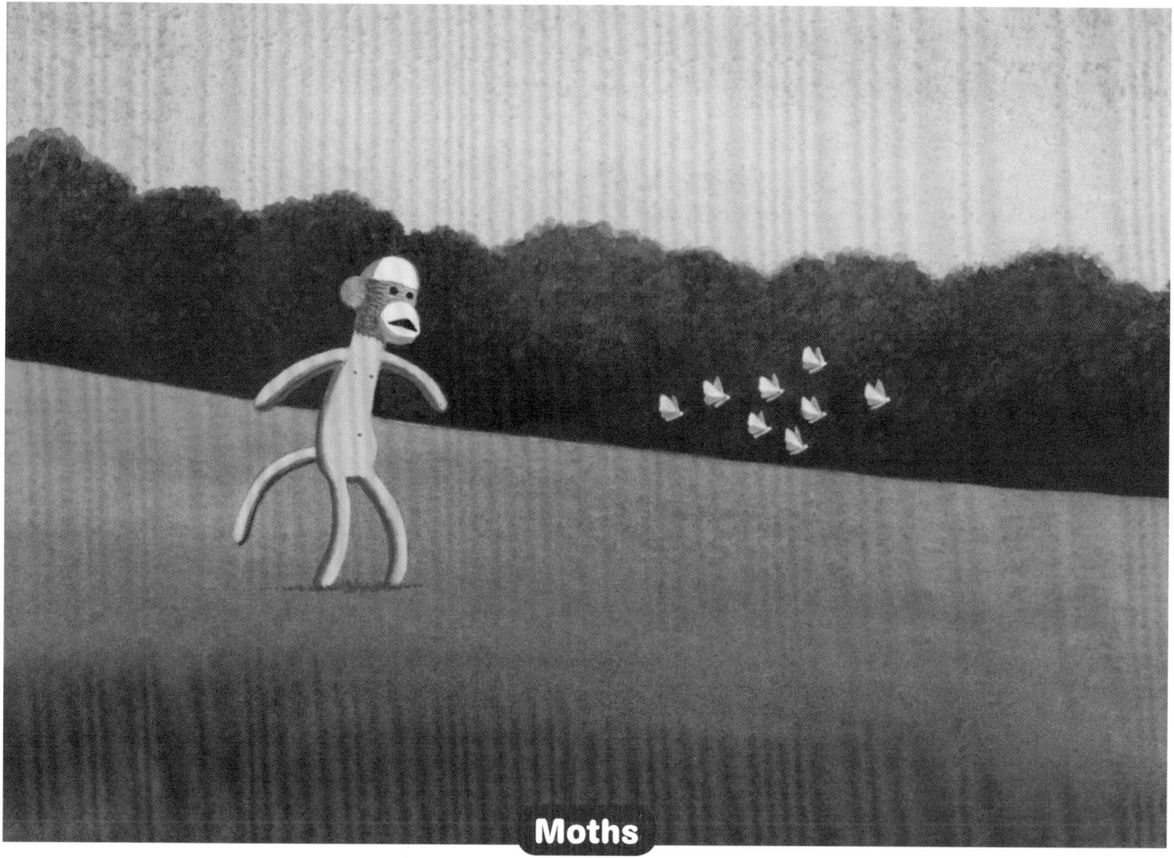
Moths

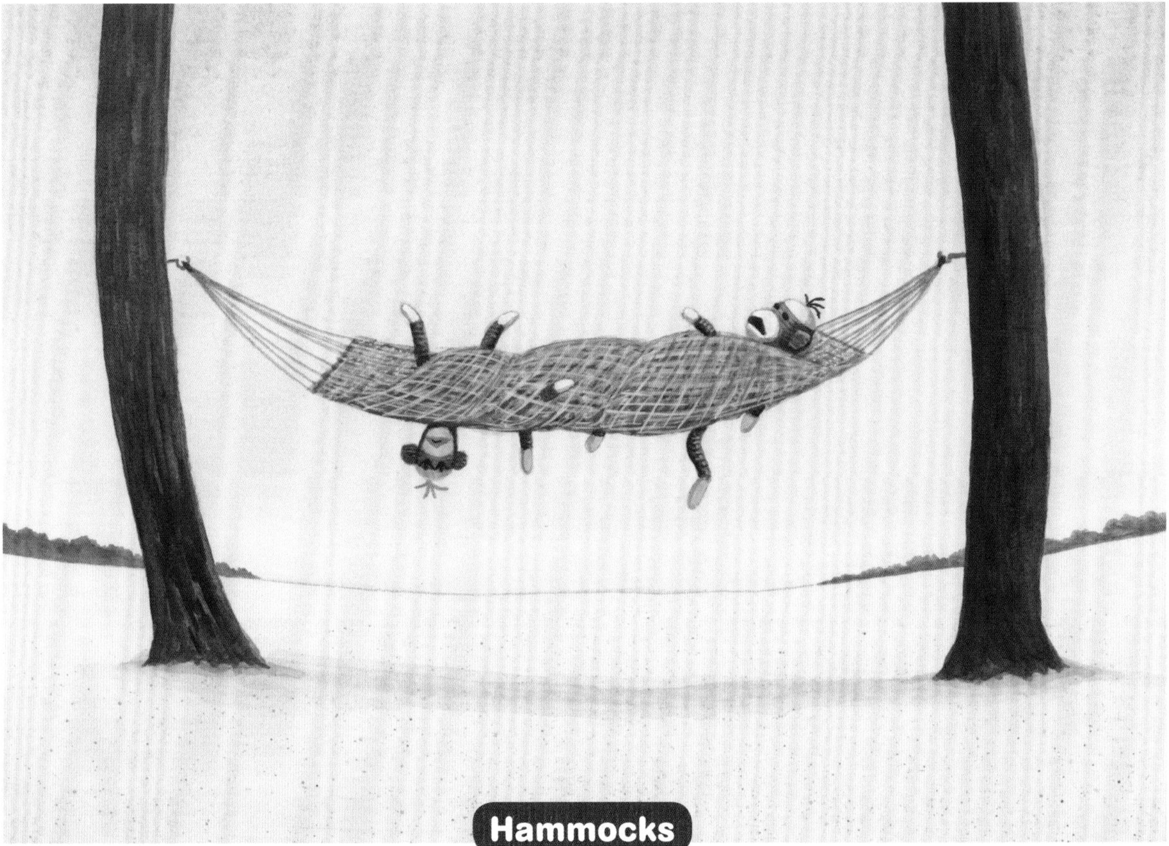

Hammocks

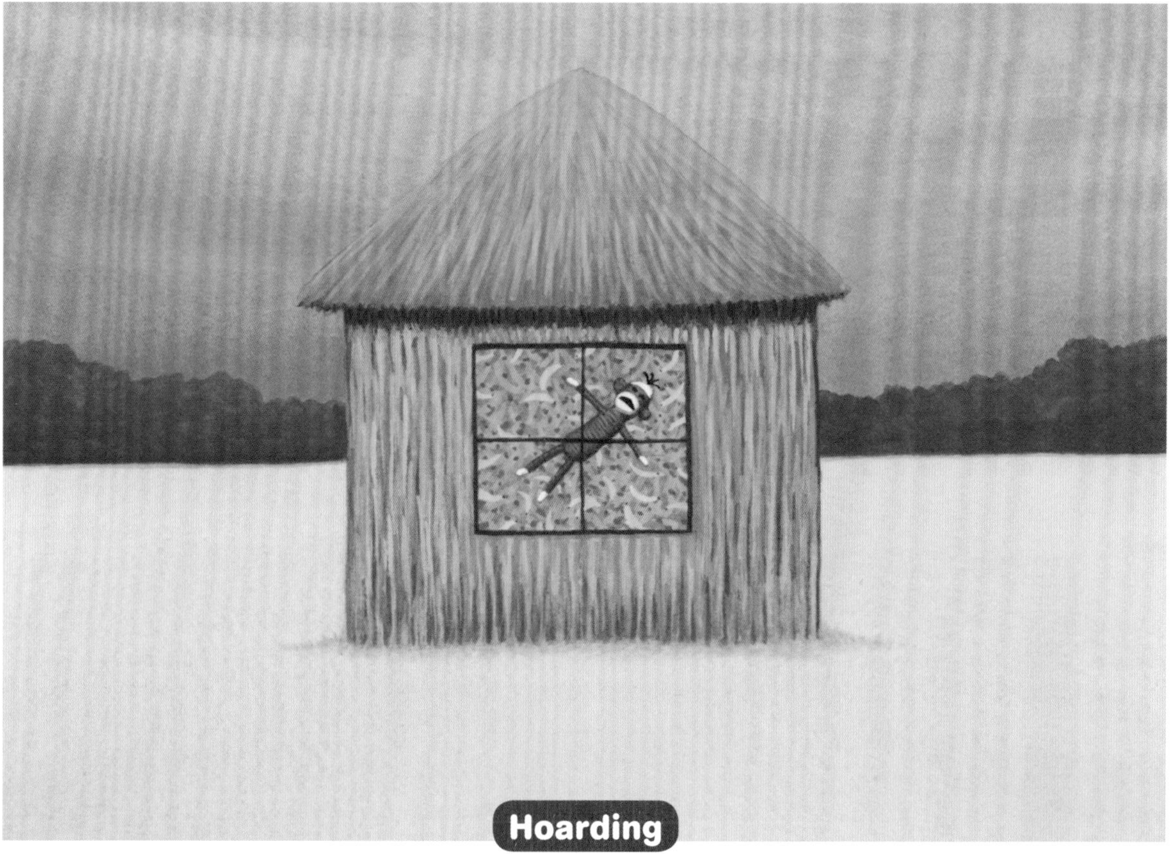

Hoarding

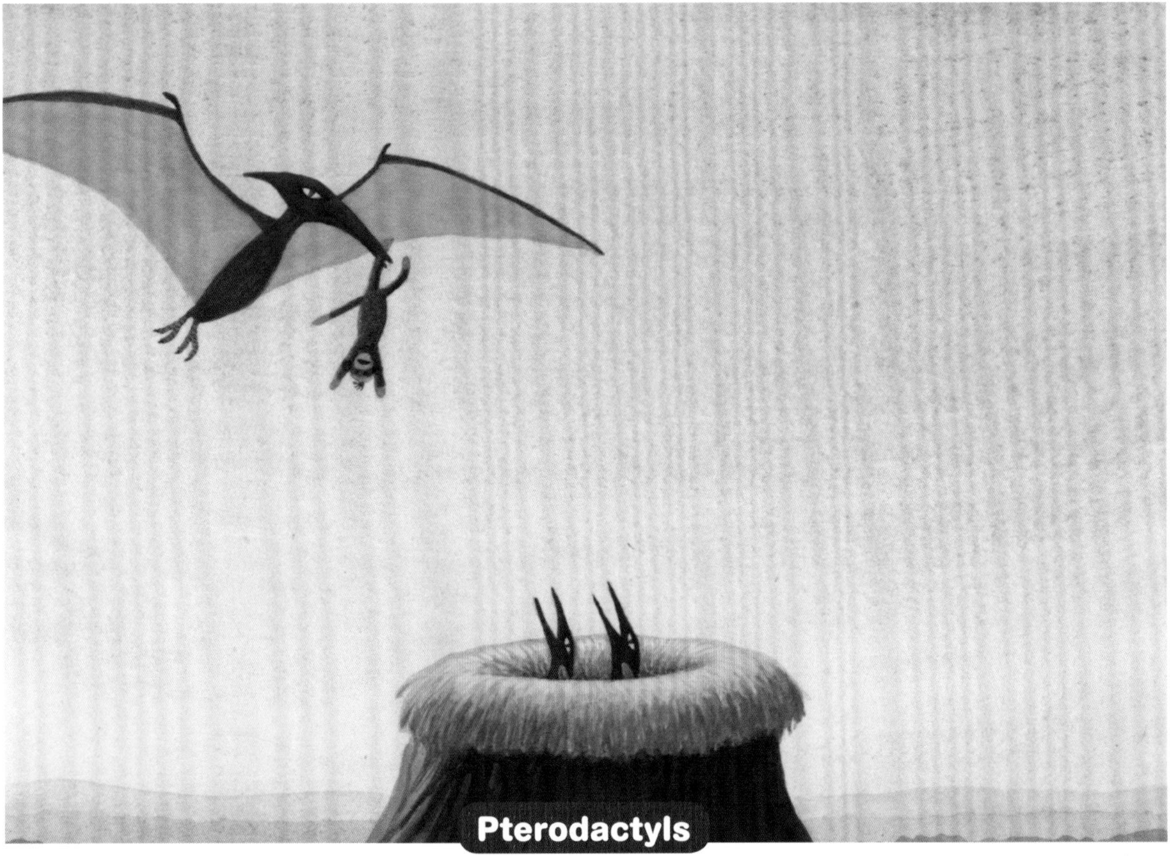
Pterodactyls

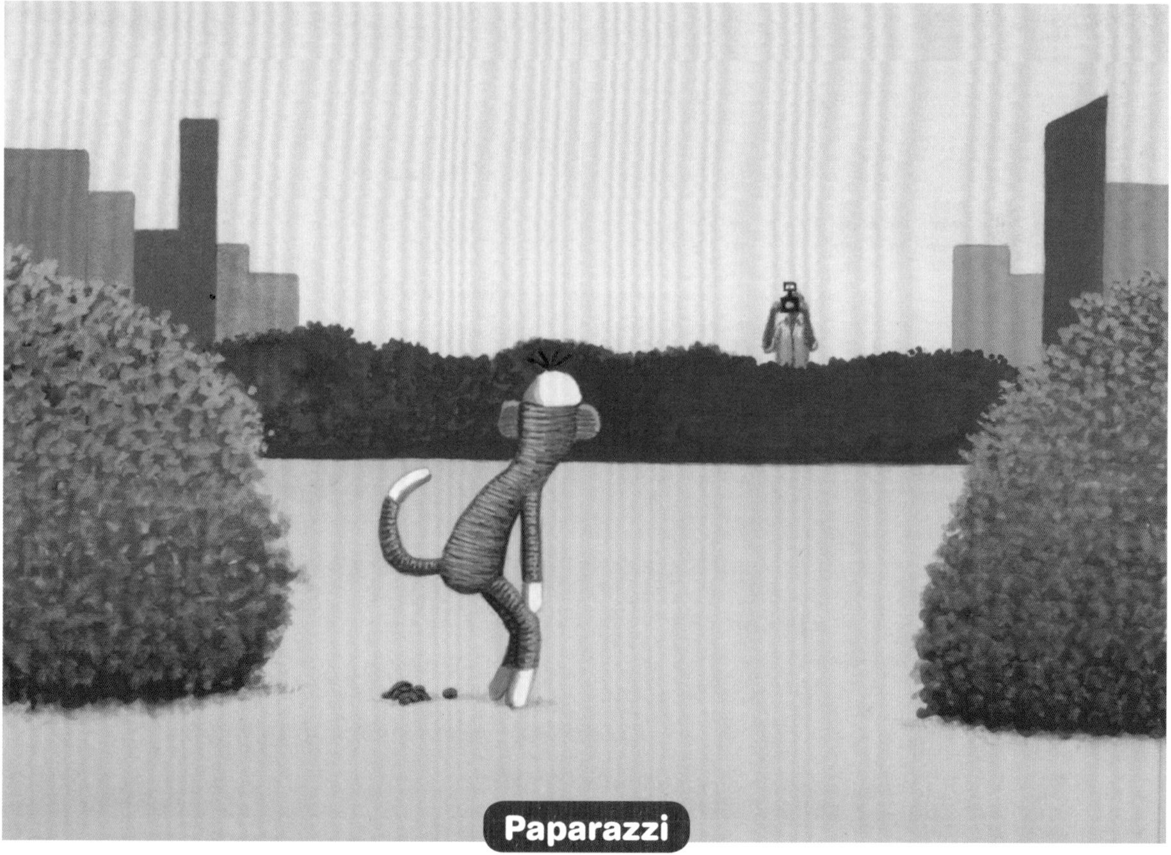

Paparazzi

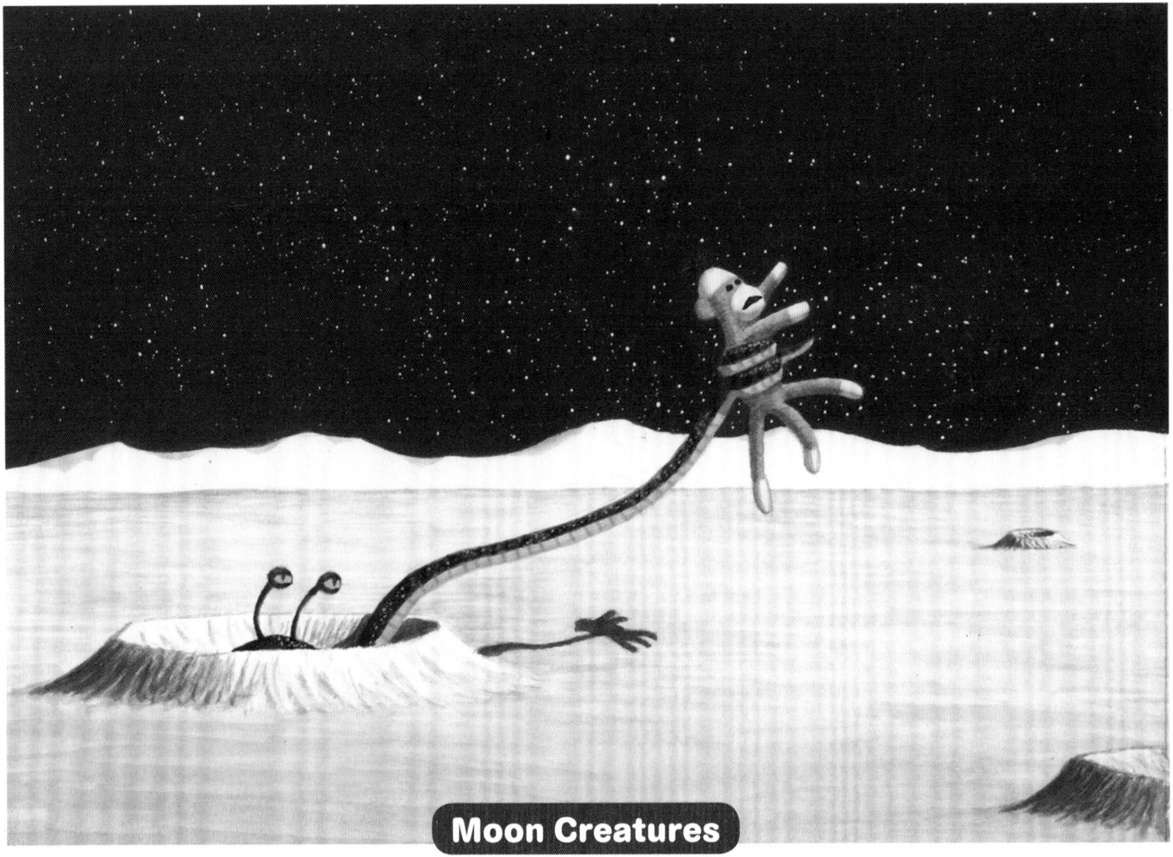

Moon Creatures

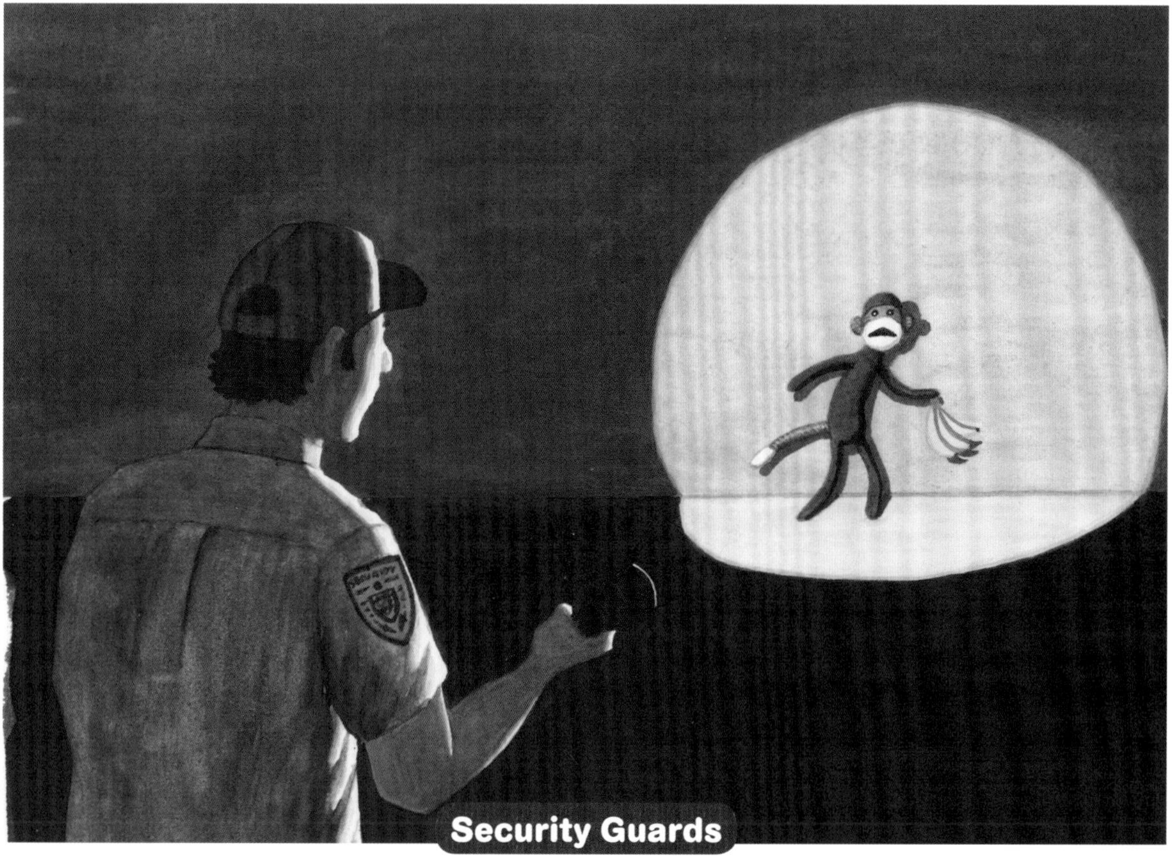

Security Guards

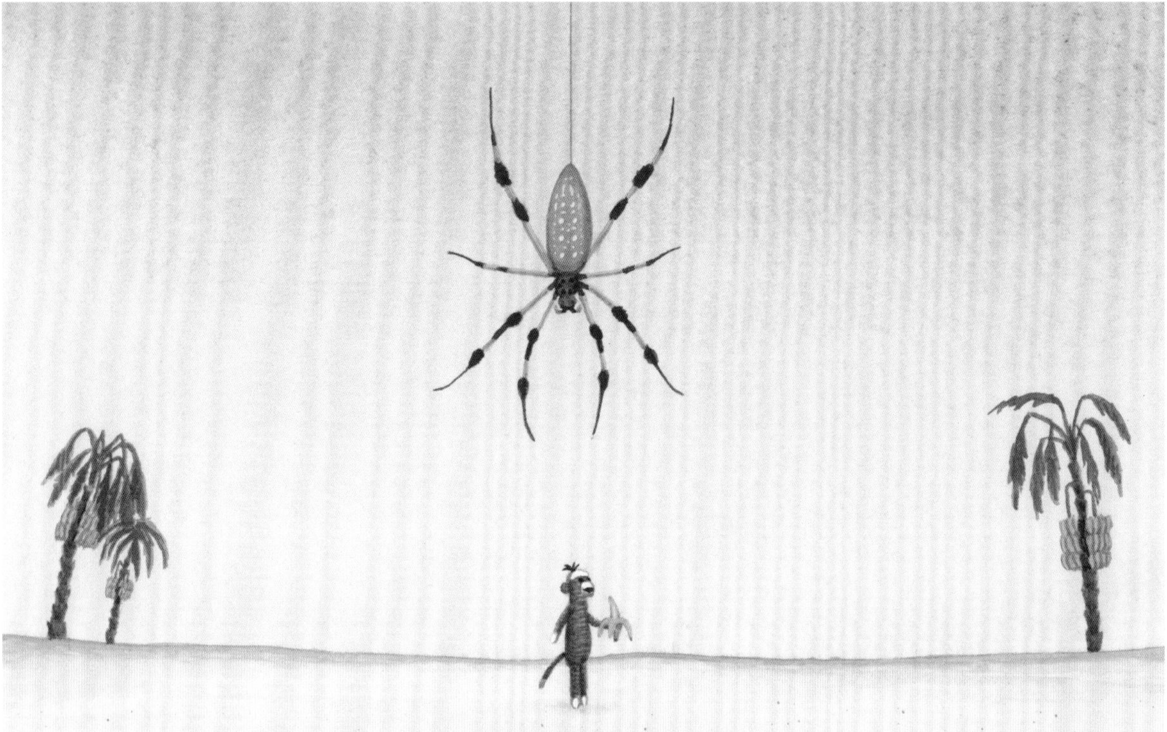

Banana Spiders

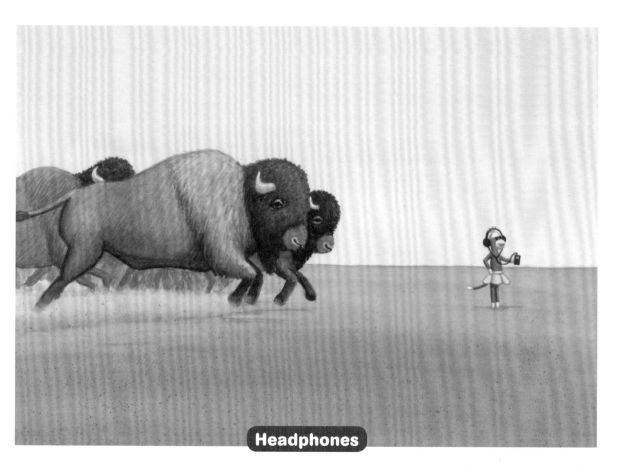

Headphones

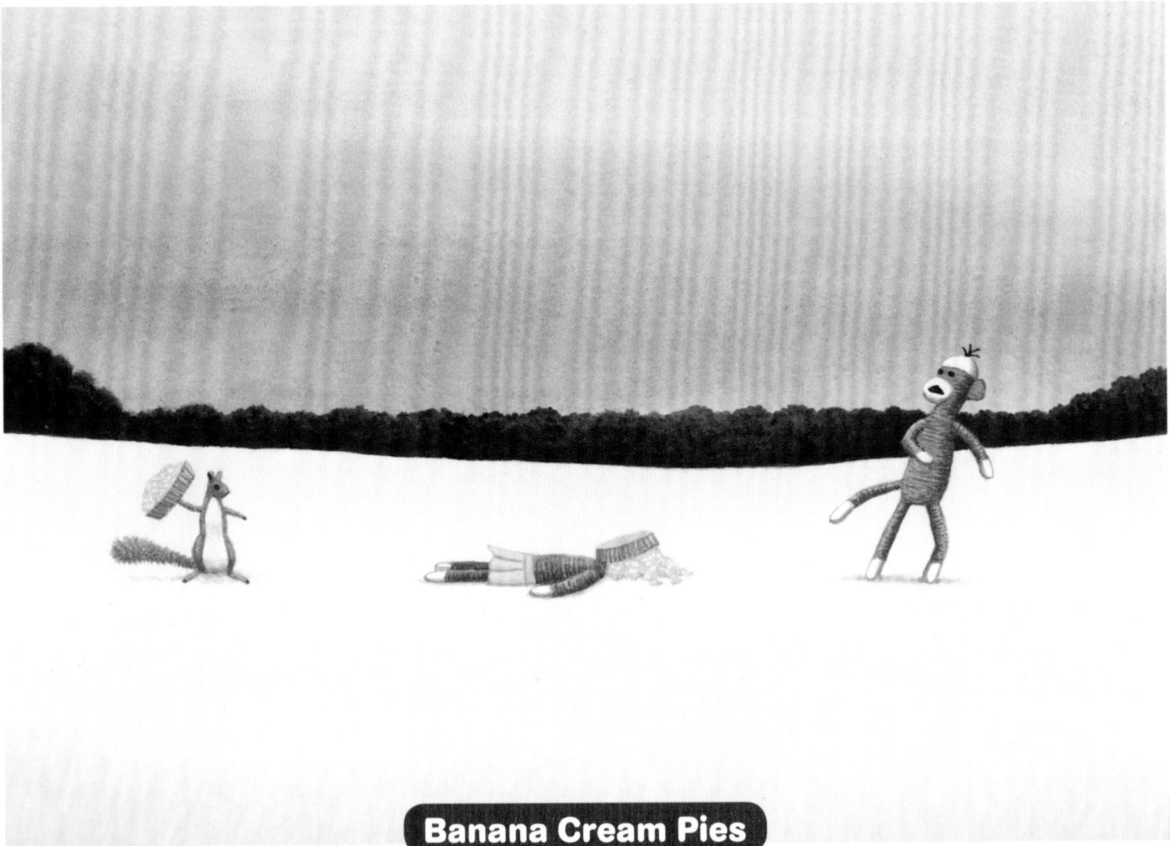

Banana Cream Pies

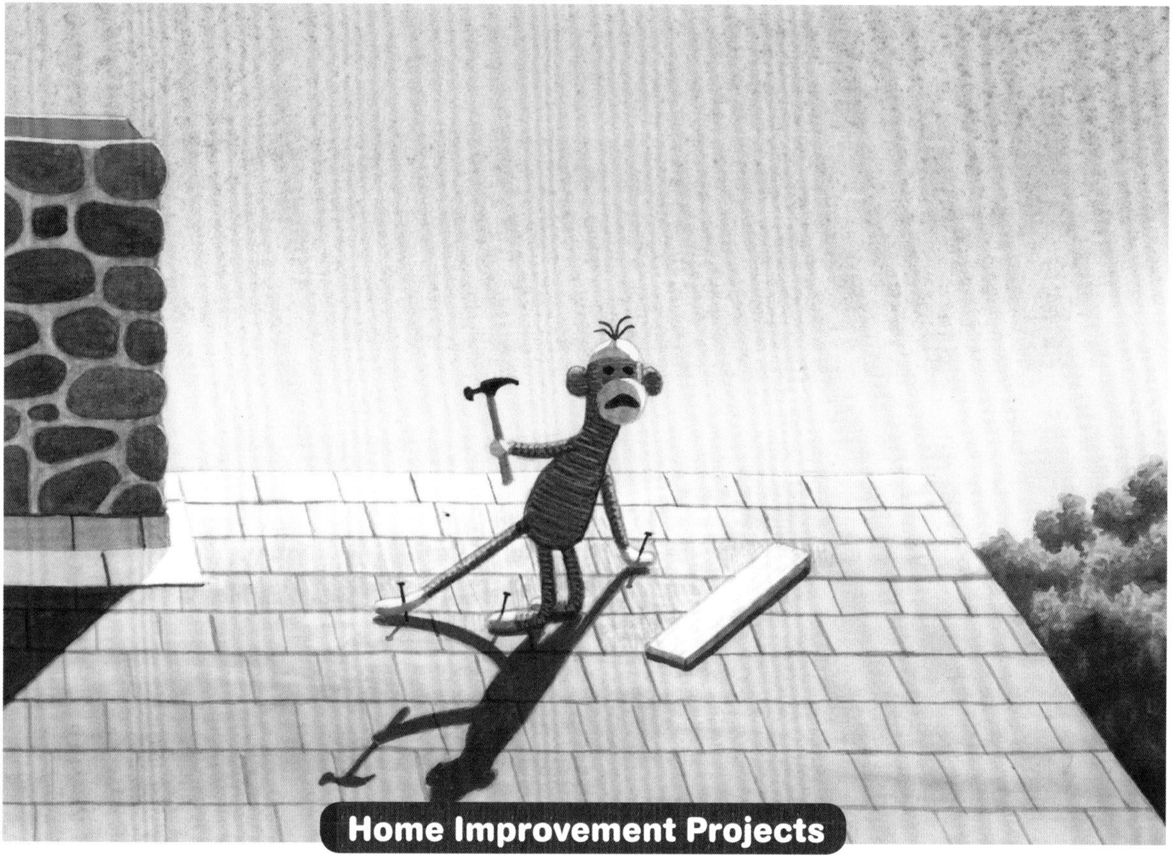
Home Improvement Projects

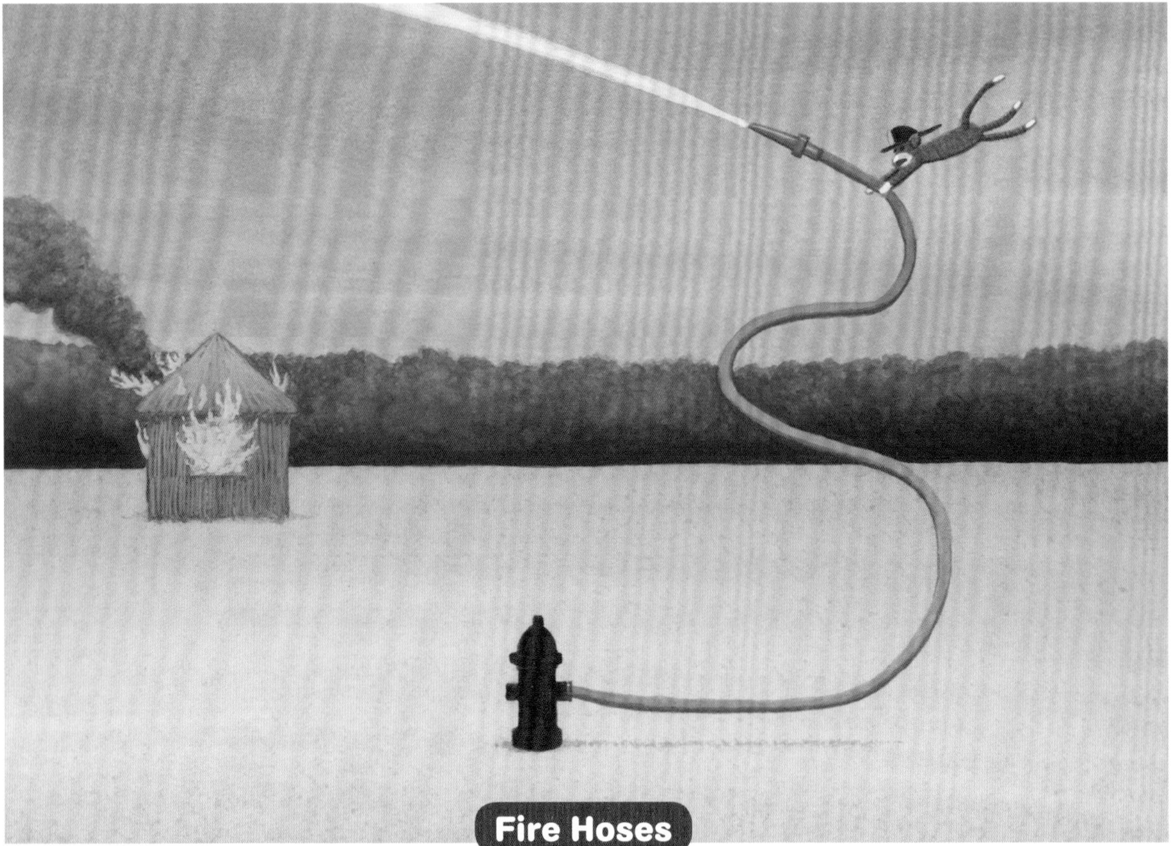

Fire Hoses

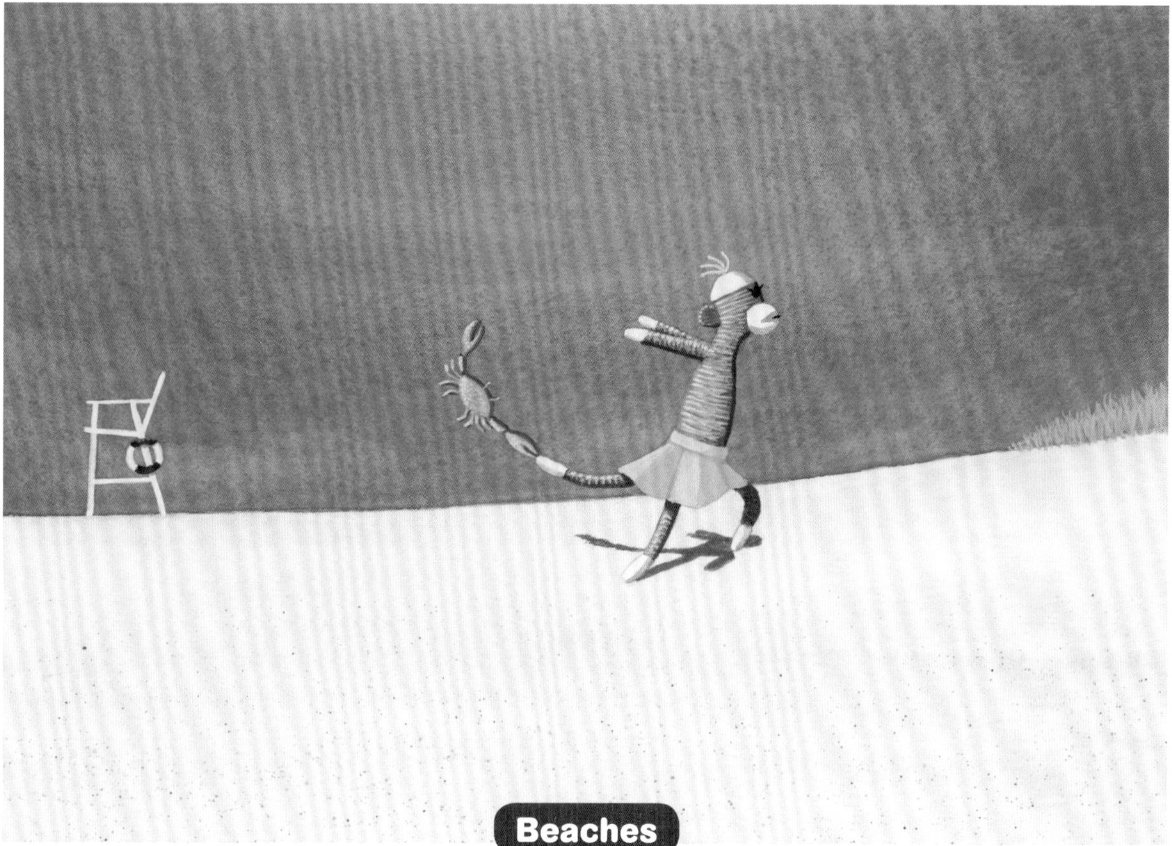

Beaches

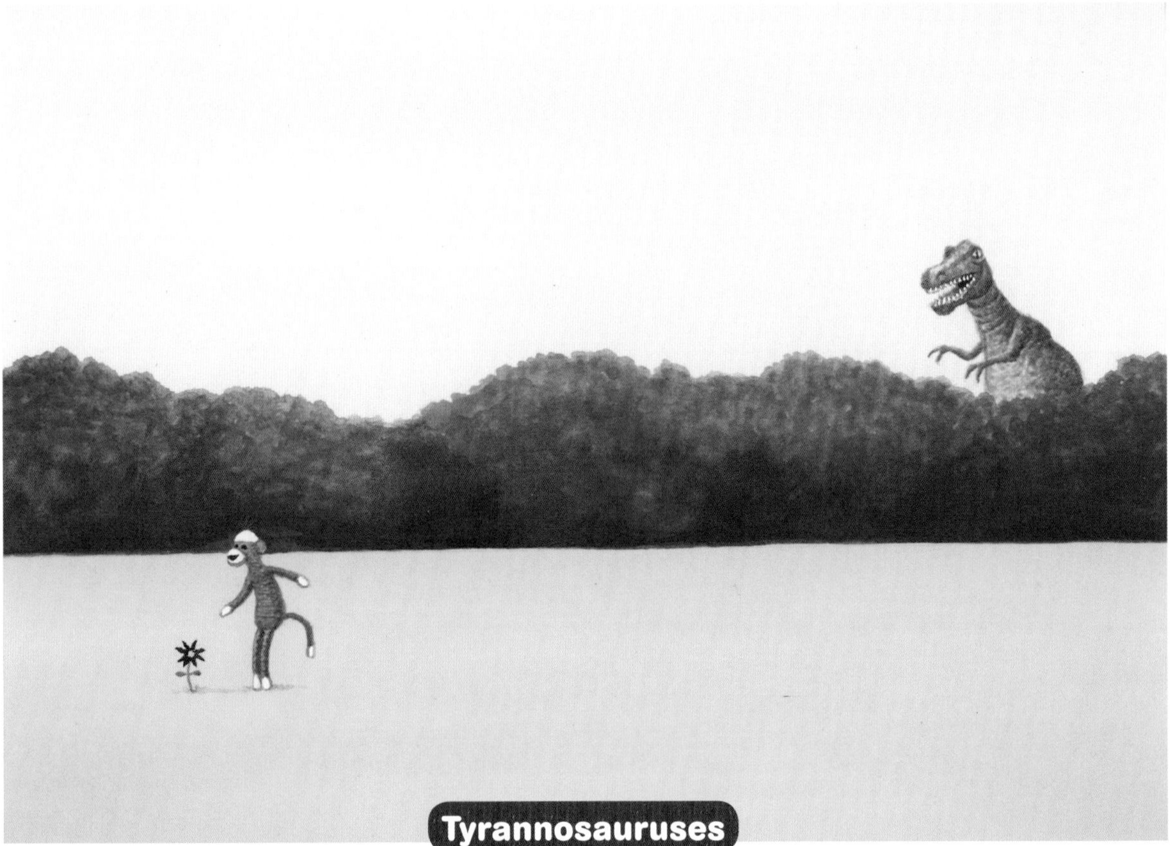

Tyrannosauruses

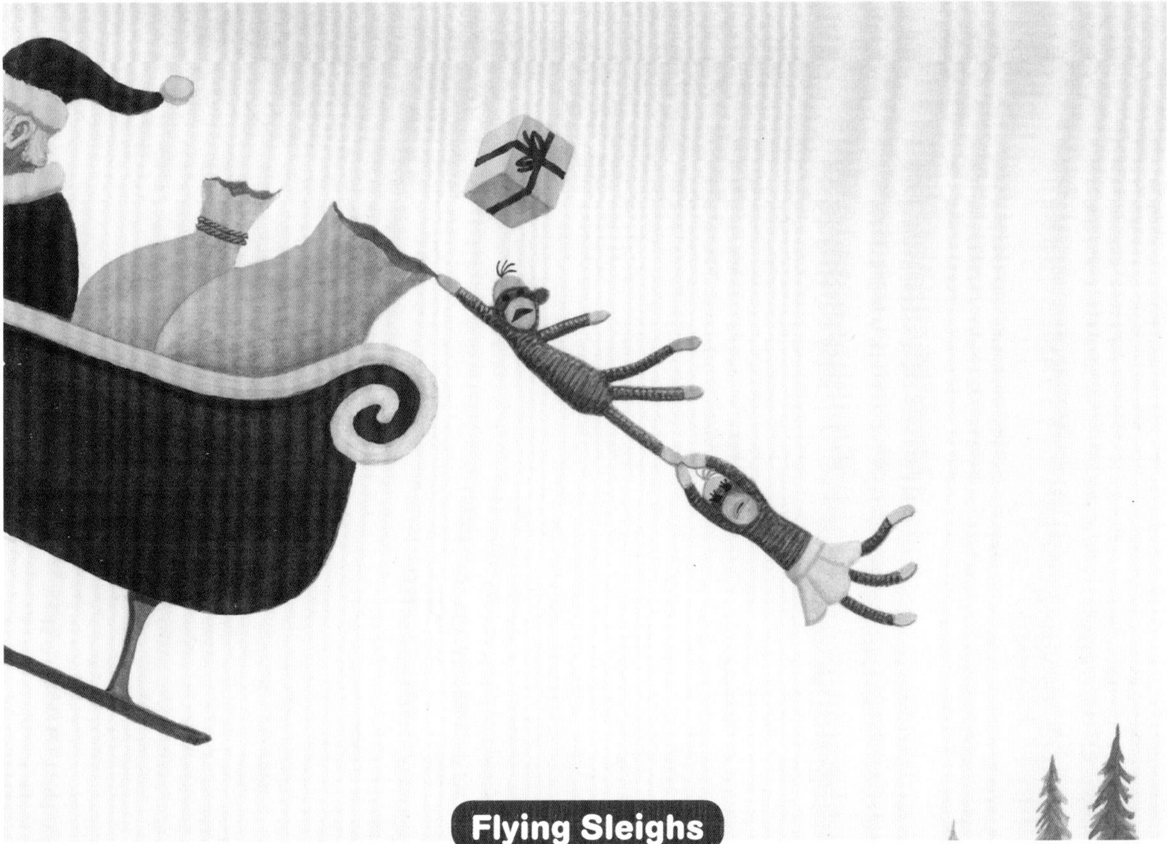
Flying Sleighs

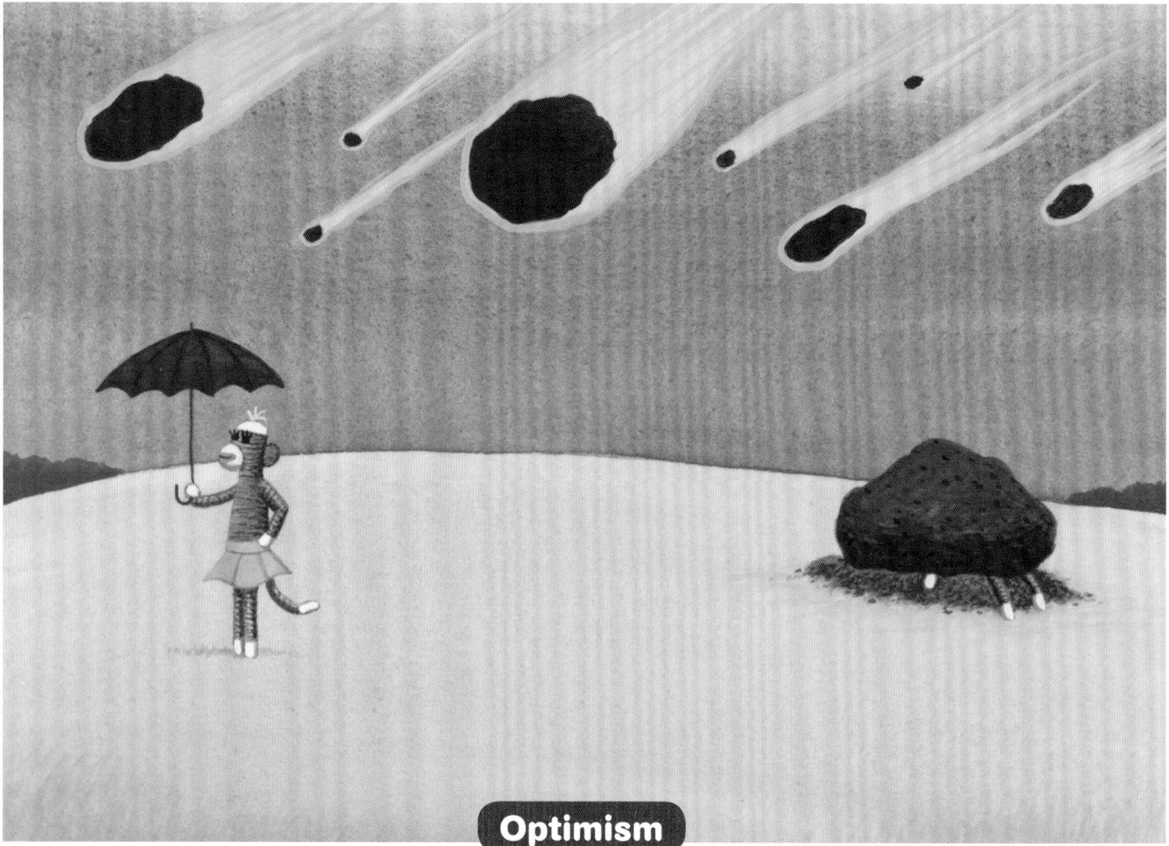
Optimism

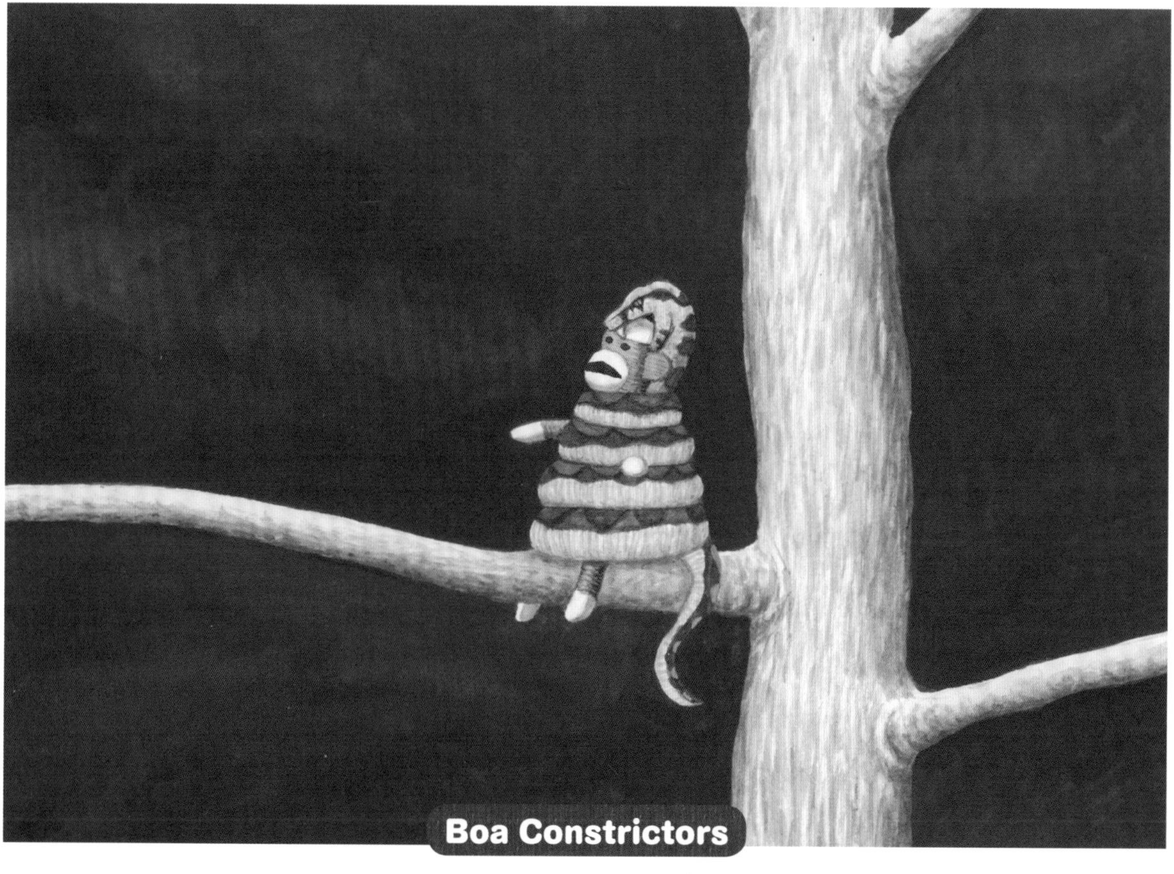

Boa Constrictors

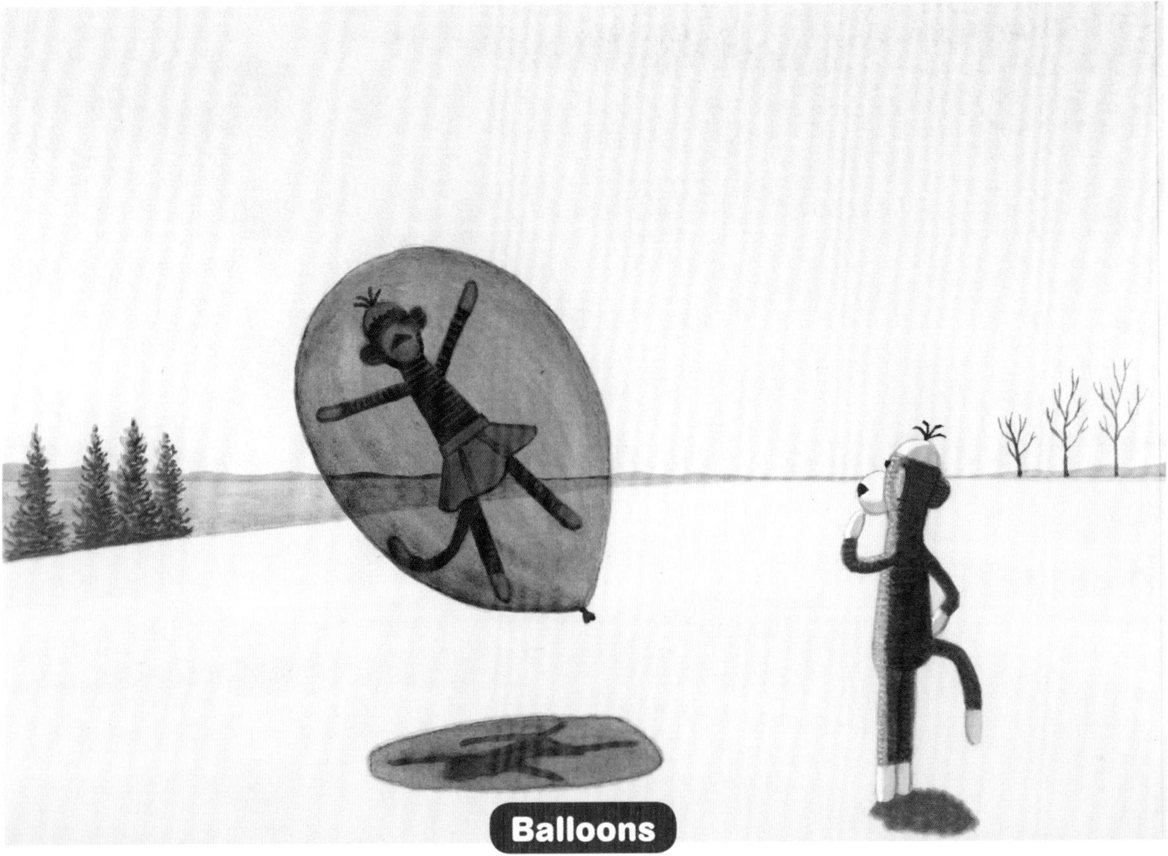

Balloons

SOCK MONKEYS REALLY LIKE . . .

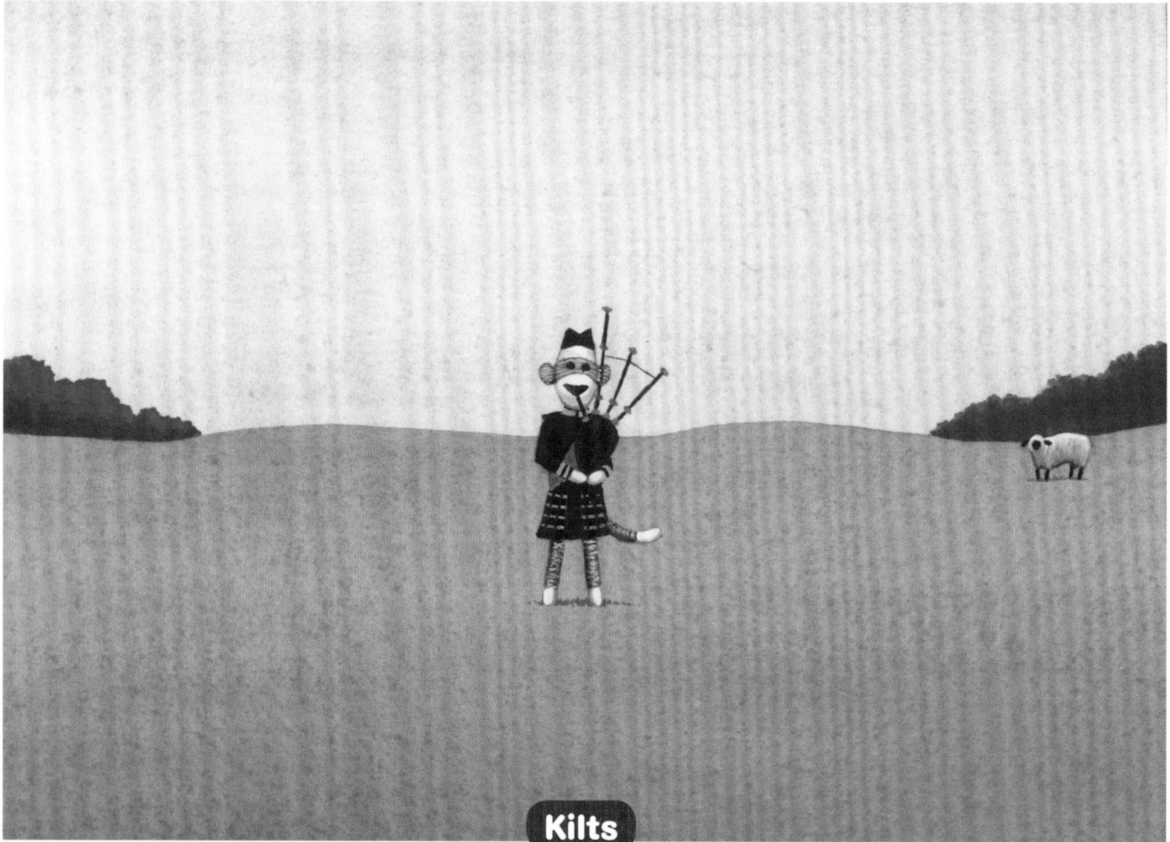

Kilts

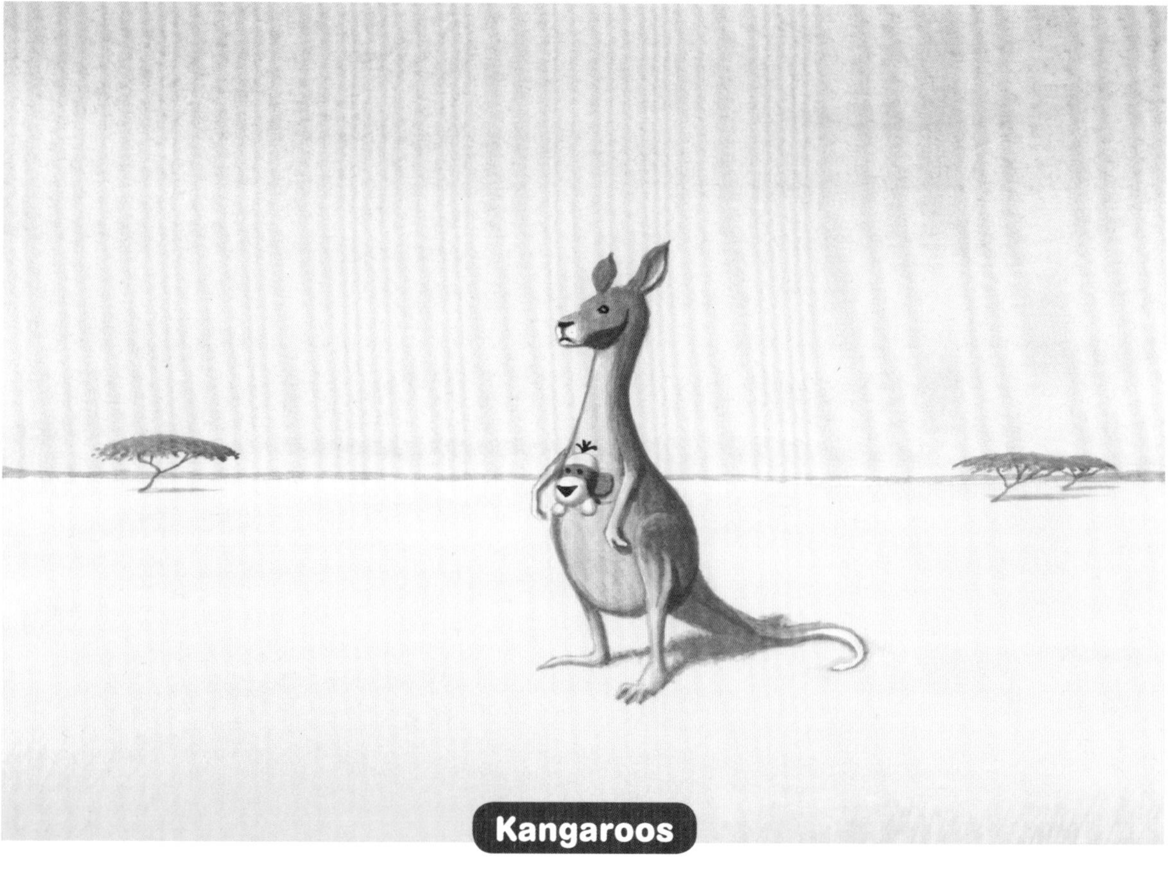
Kangaroos

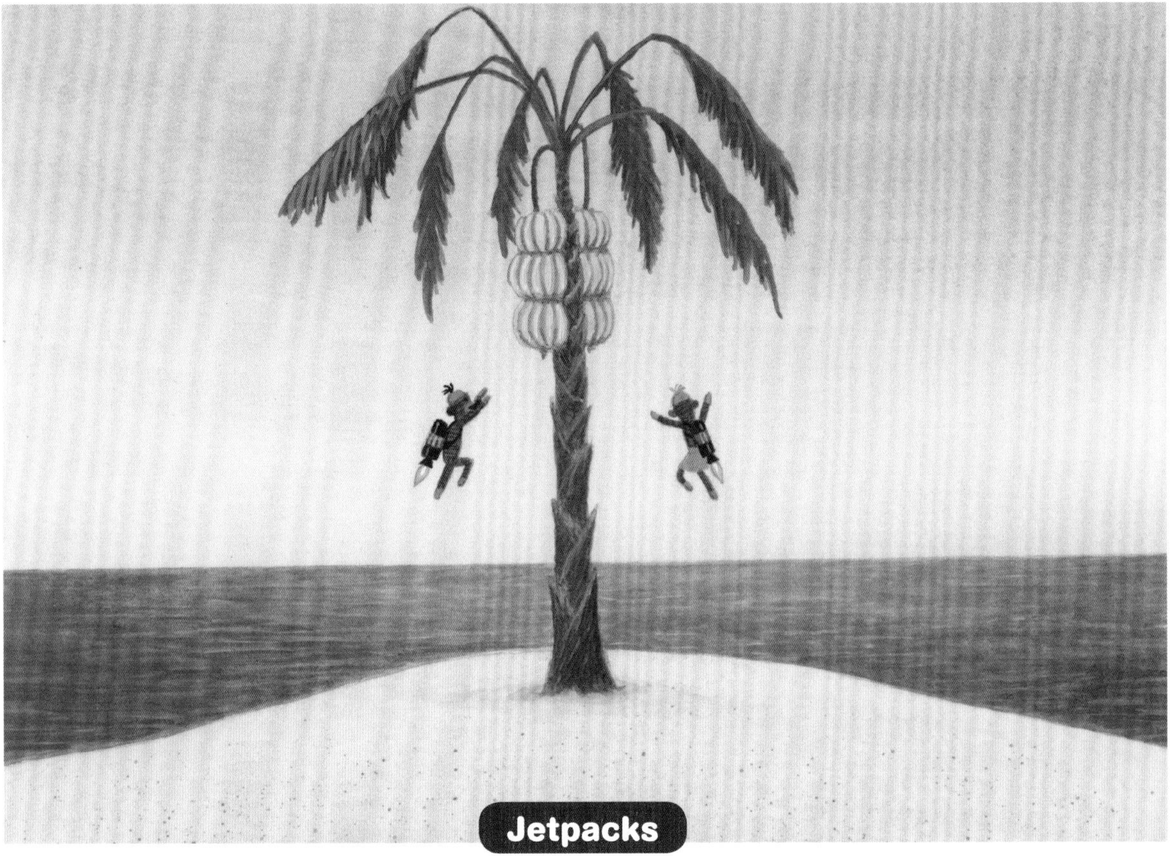
Jetpacks

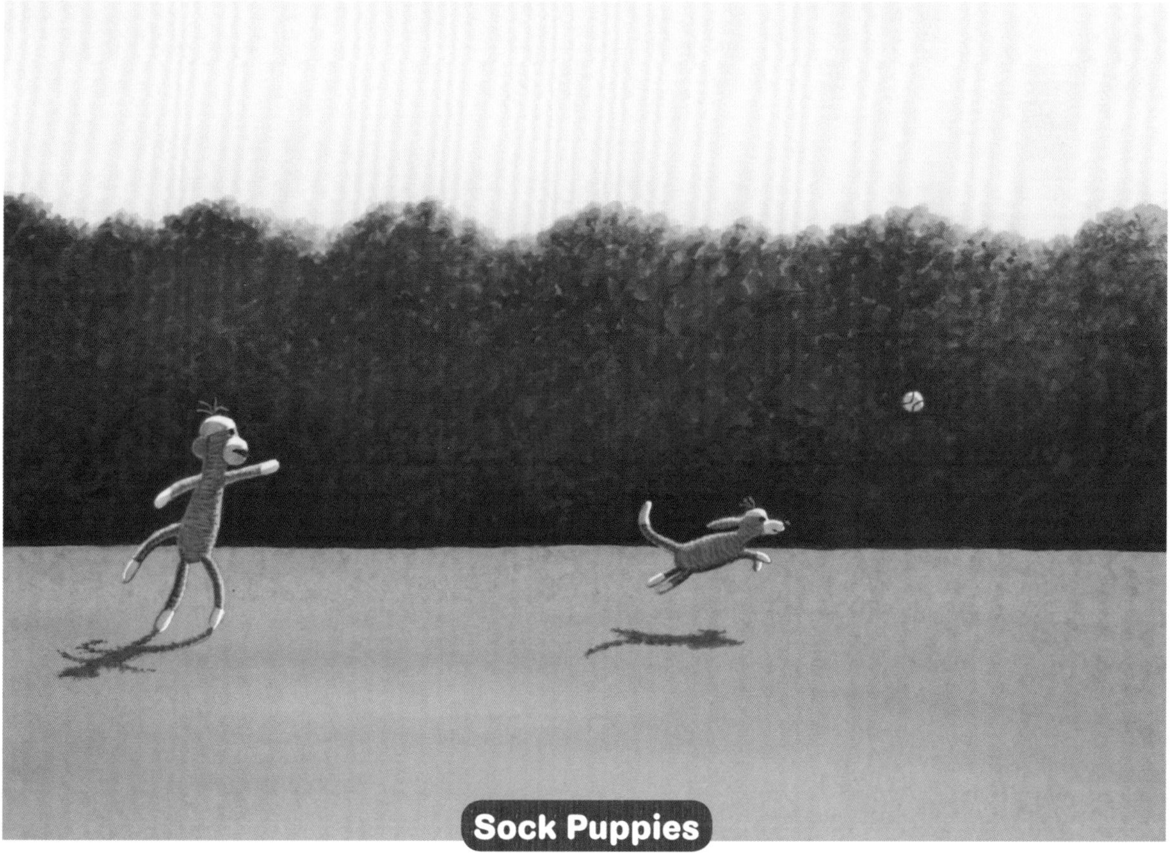
Sock Puppies

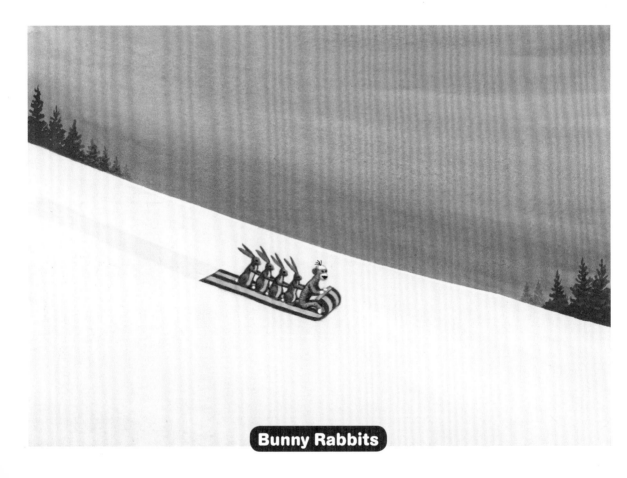

Bunny Rabbits

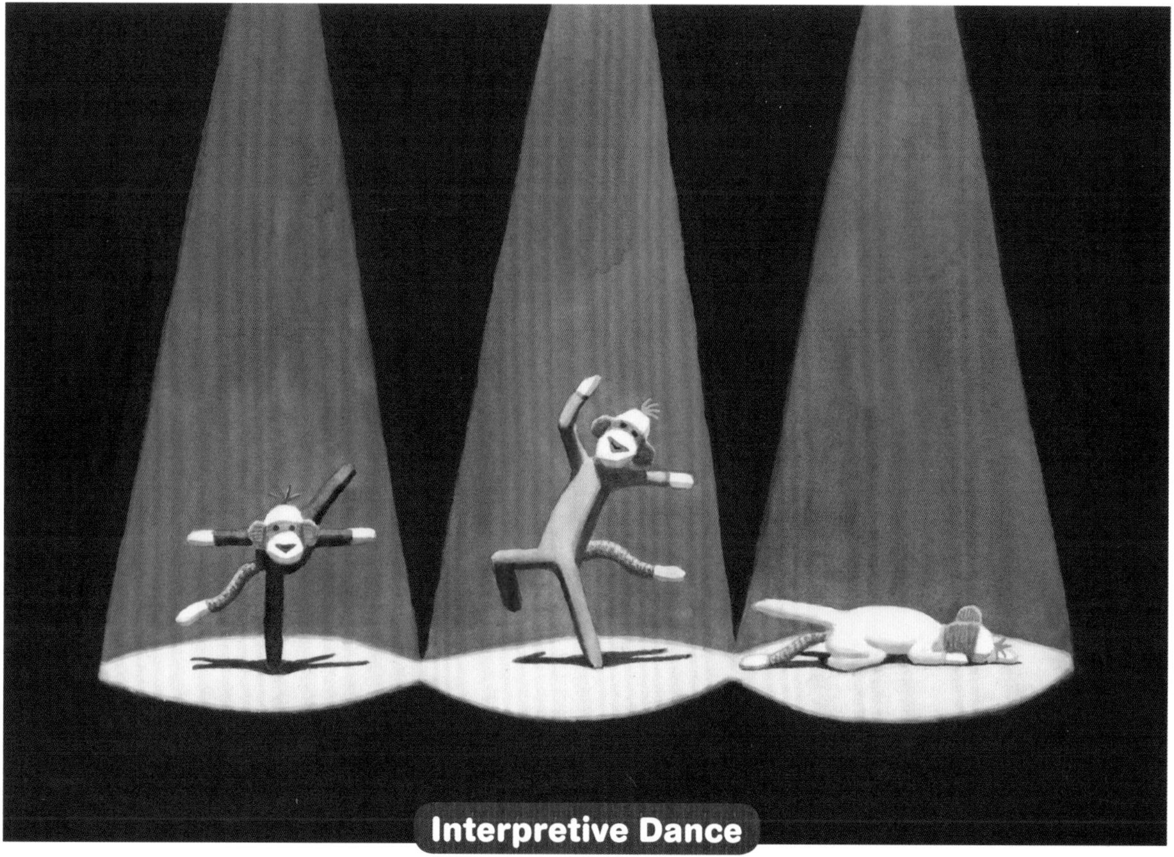

Interpretive Dance

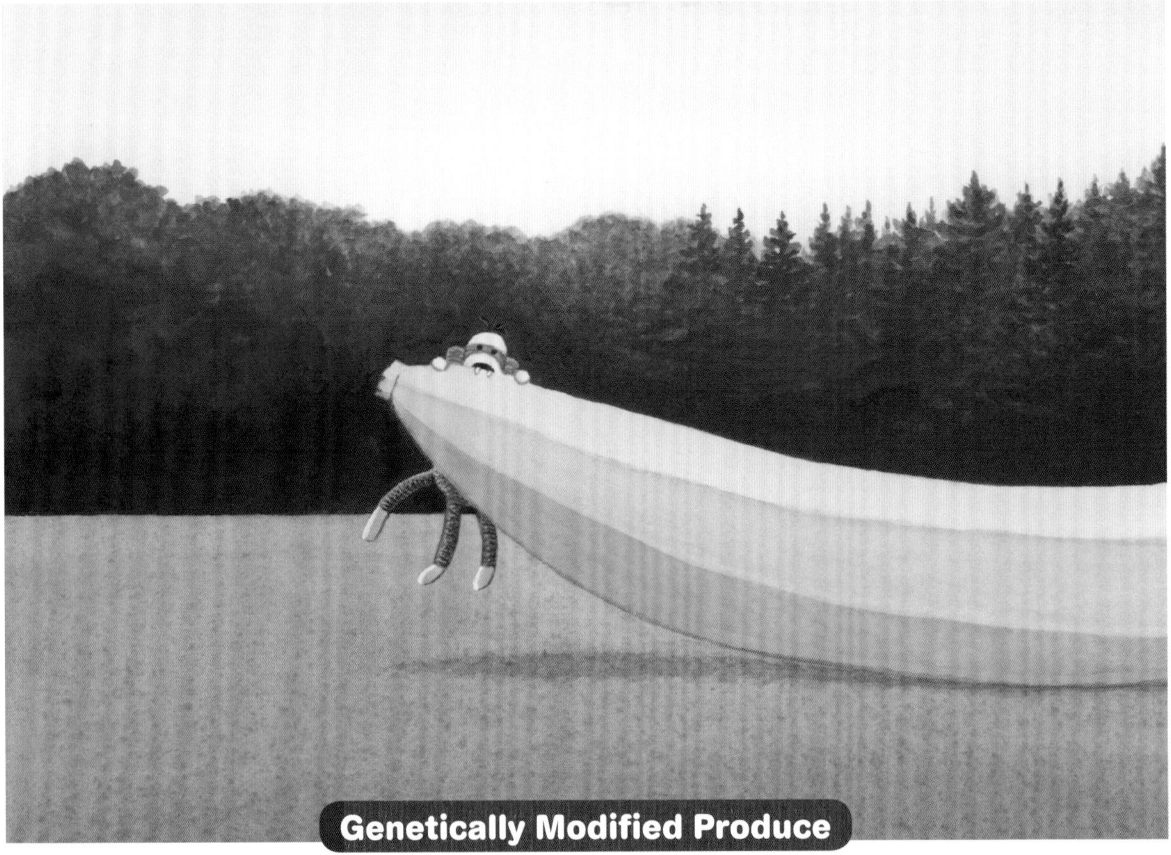

Genetically Modified Produce

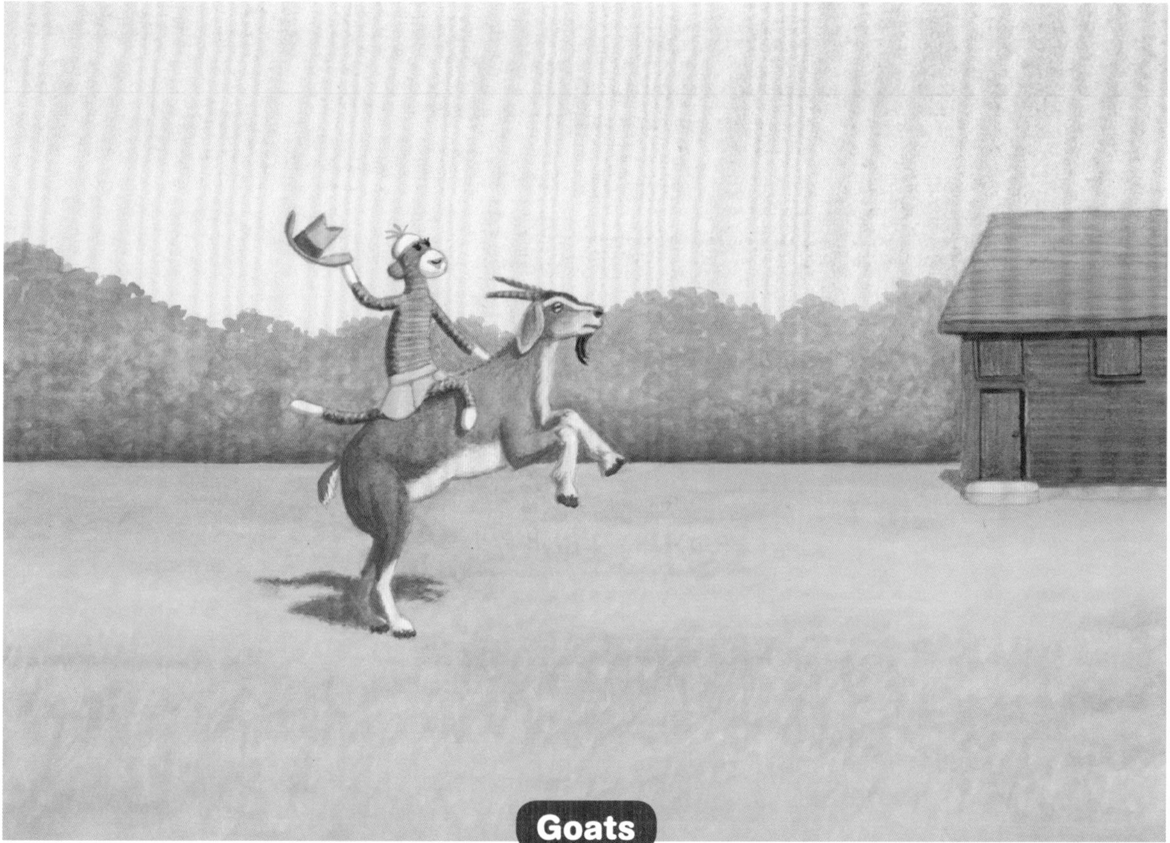

Goats

5000 B.C.
1589 A.D.
1932 A.D.
2277 A.D.

Progress

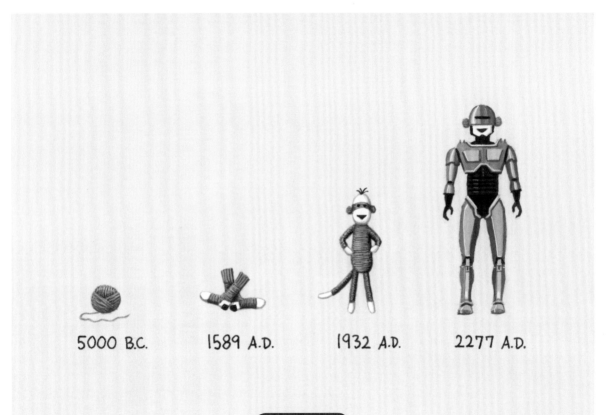

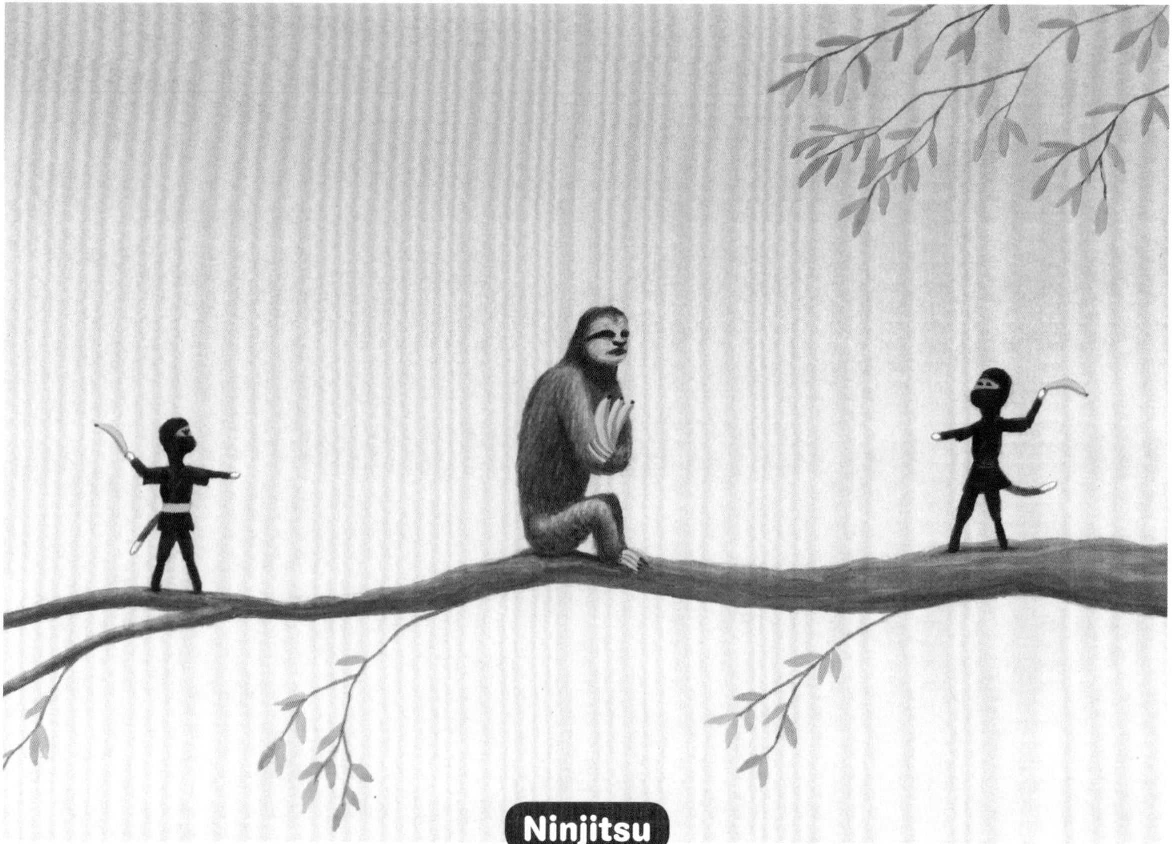

Ninjitsu

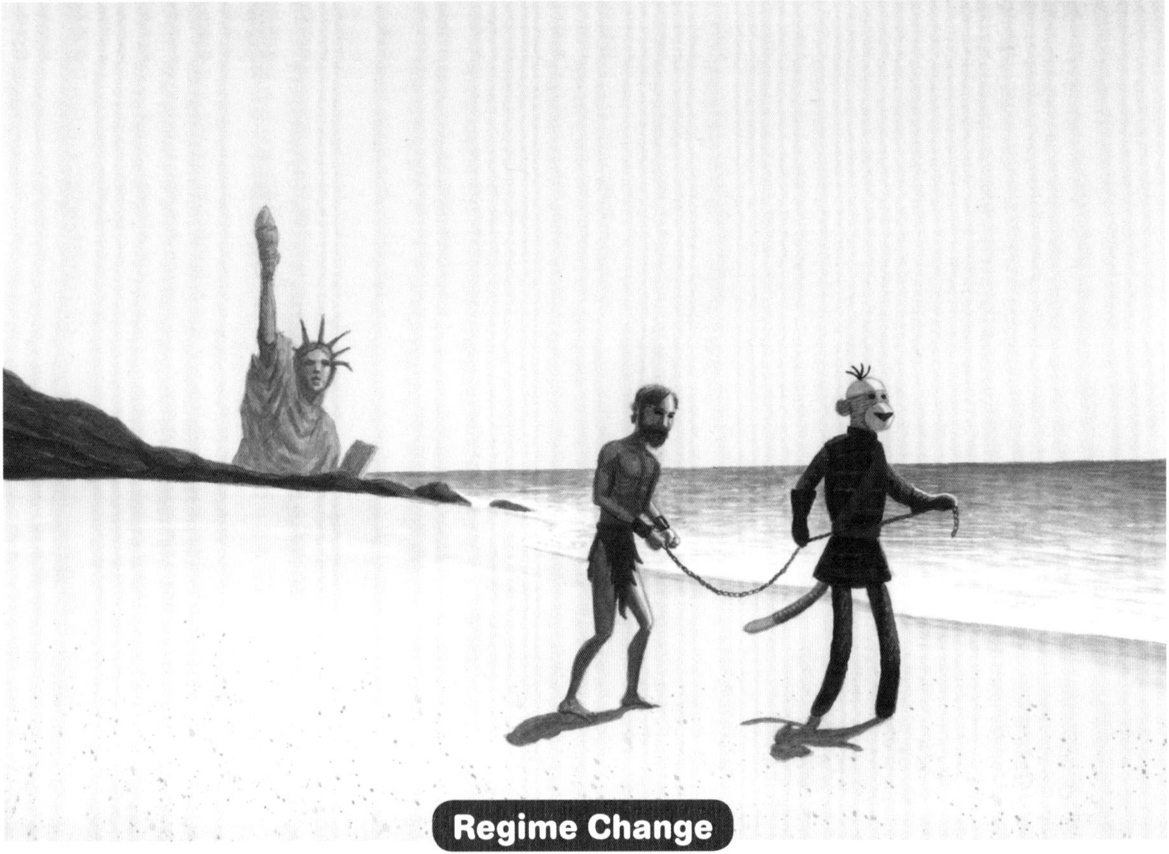

Regime Change

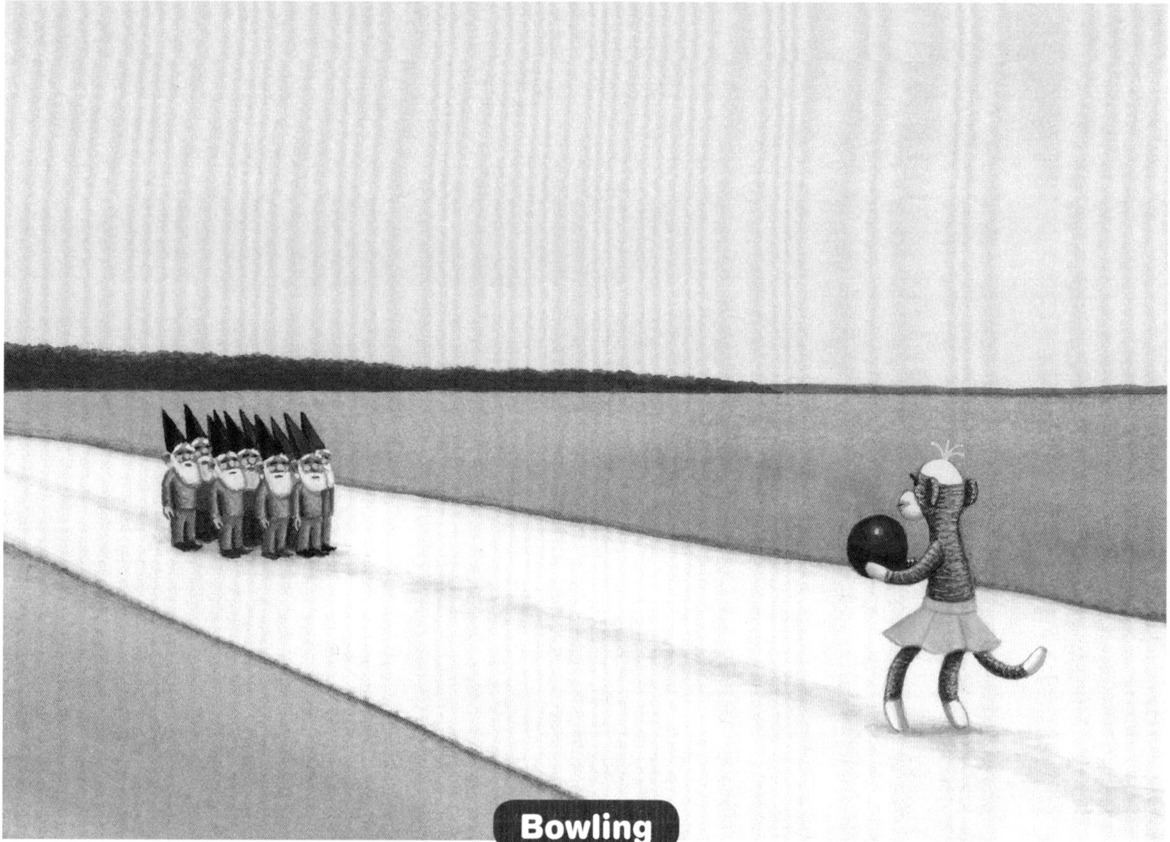

Bowling

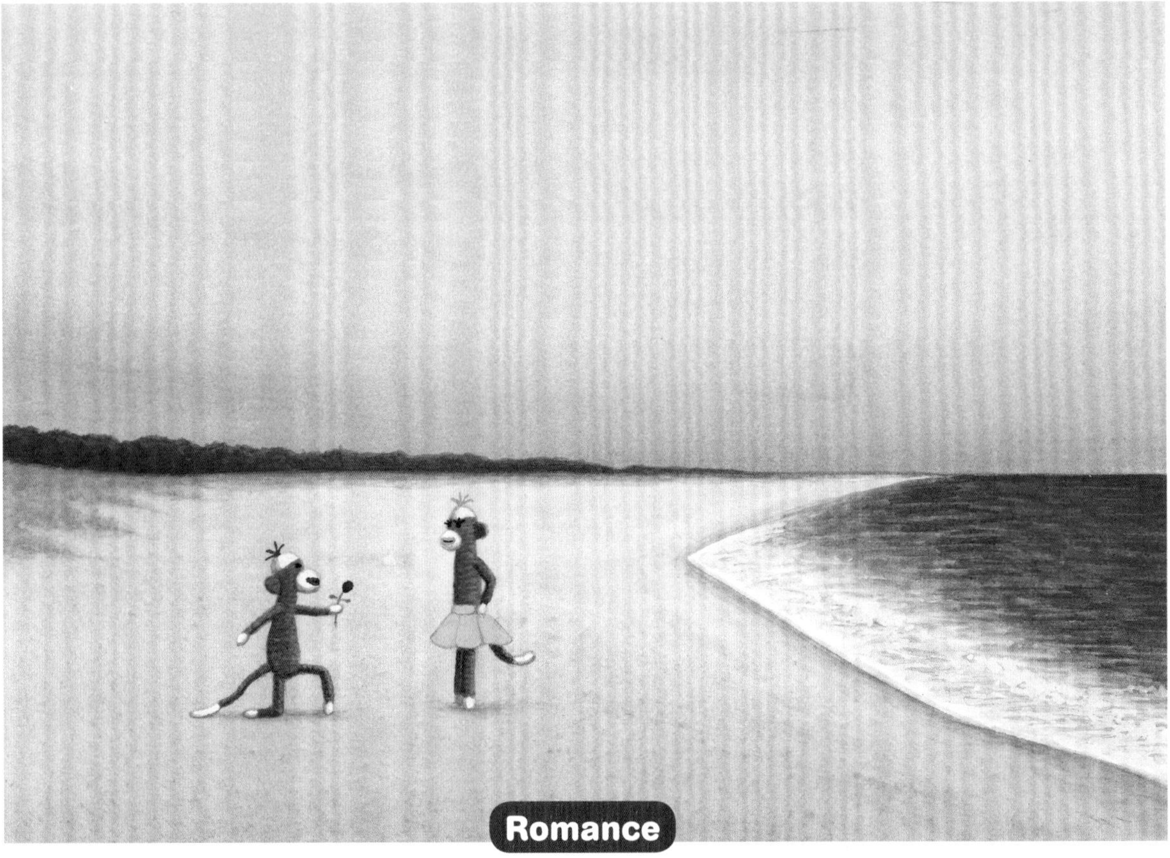

Romance

SOCK MONKEYS HAVE MAJOR ISSUES WITH . . .

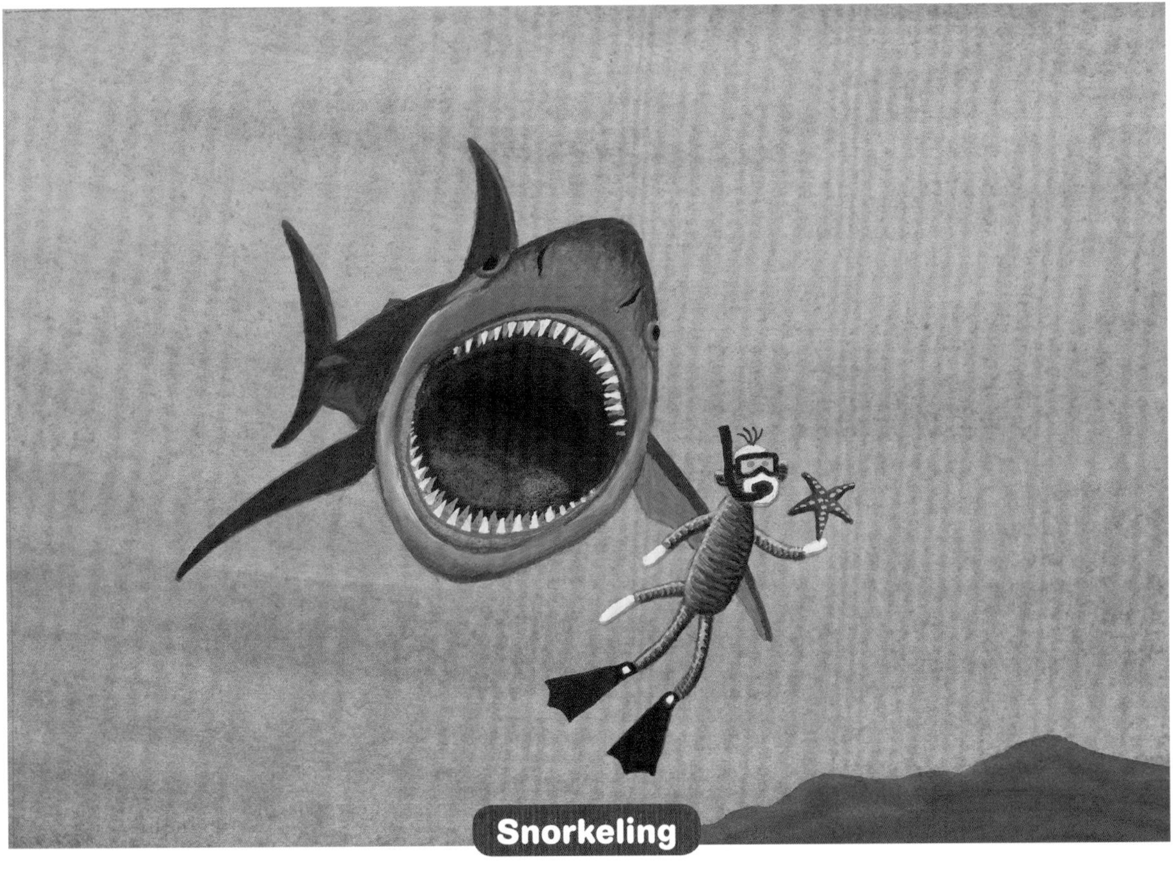
Snorkeling

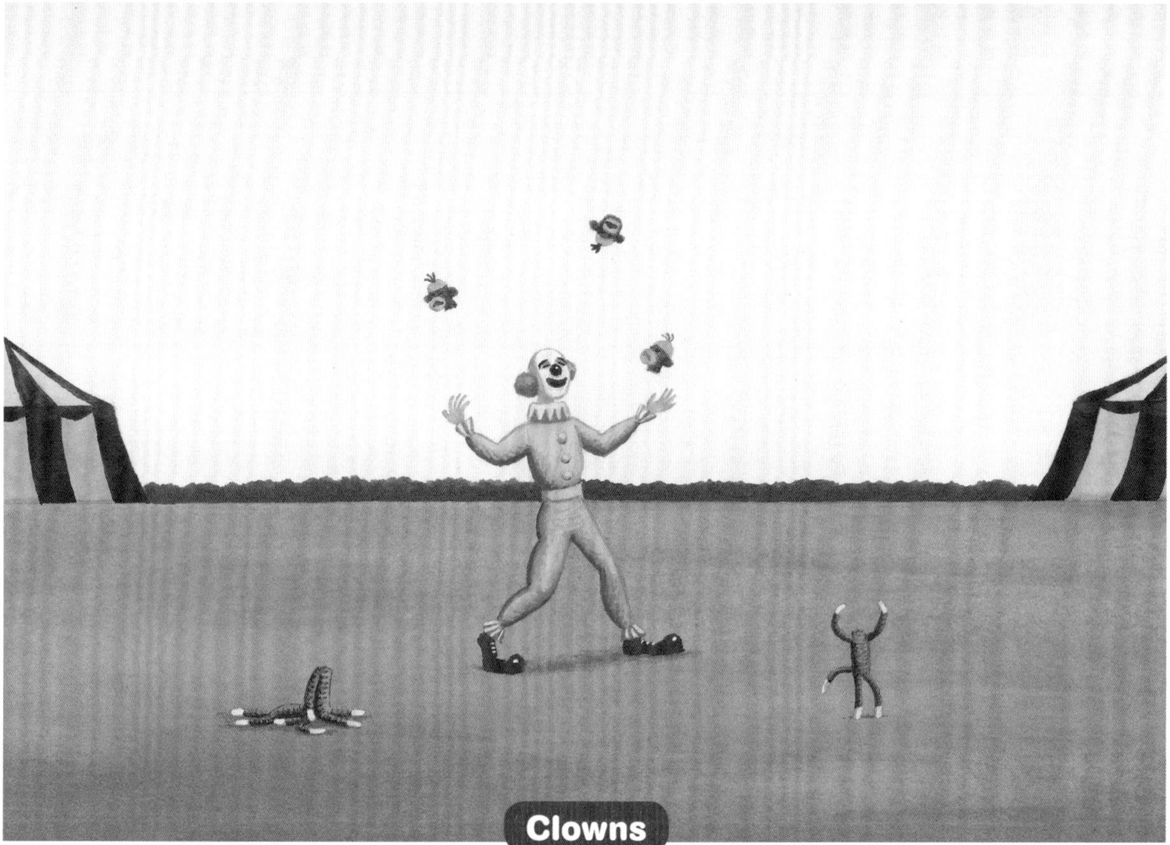

Clowns

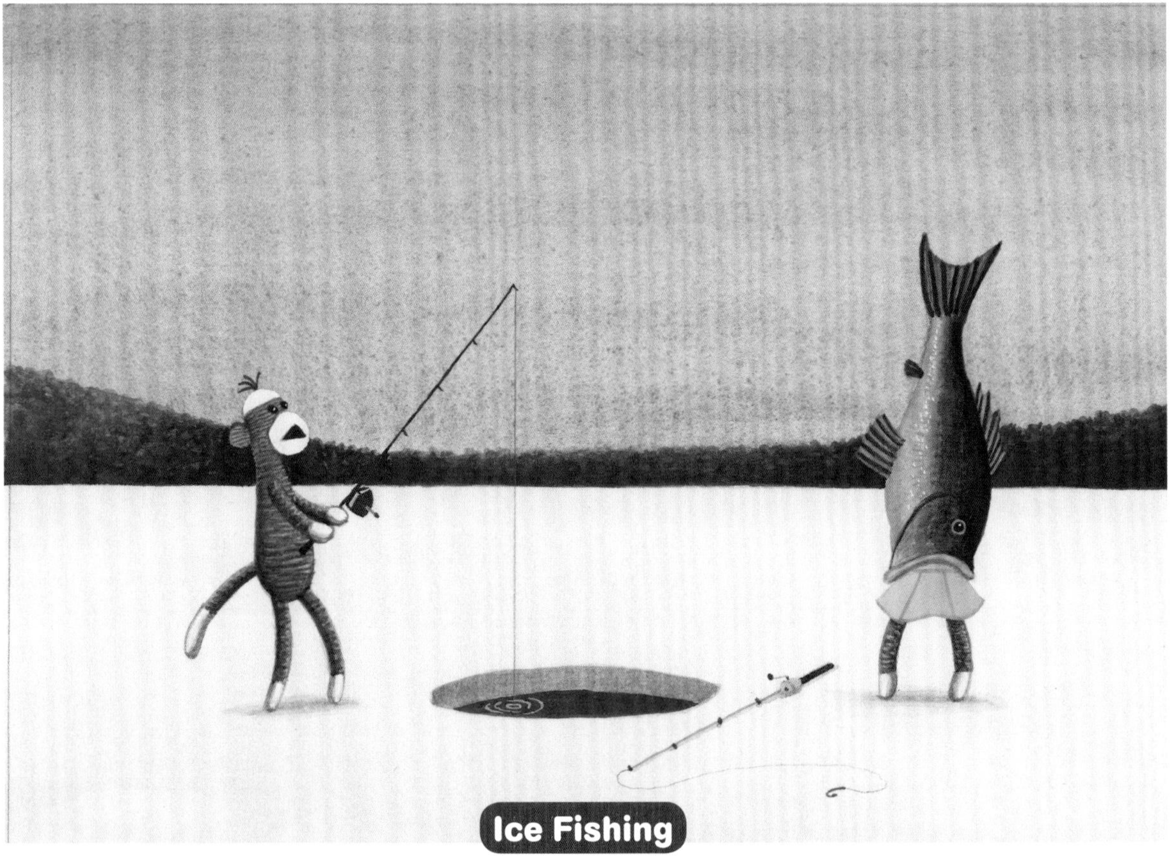

Ice Fishing

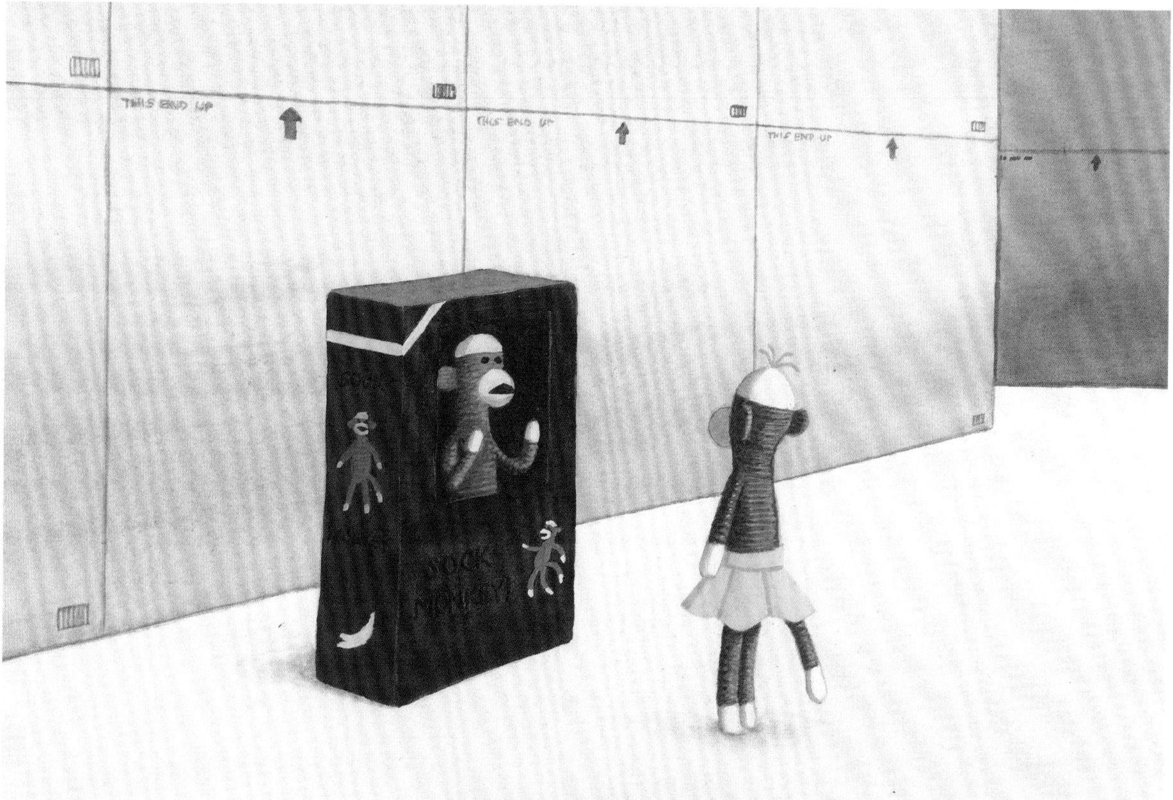
THIS END UP
SOCK MONKEY!

Confined Spaces

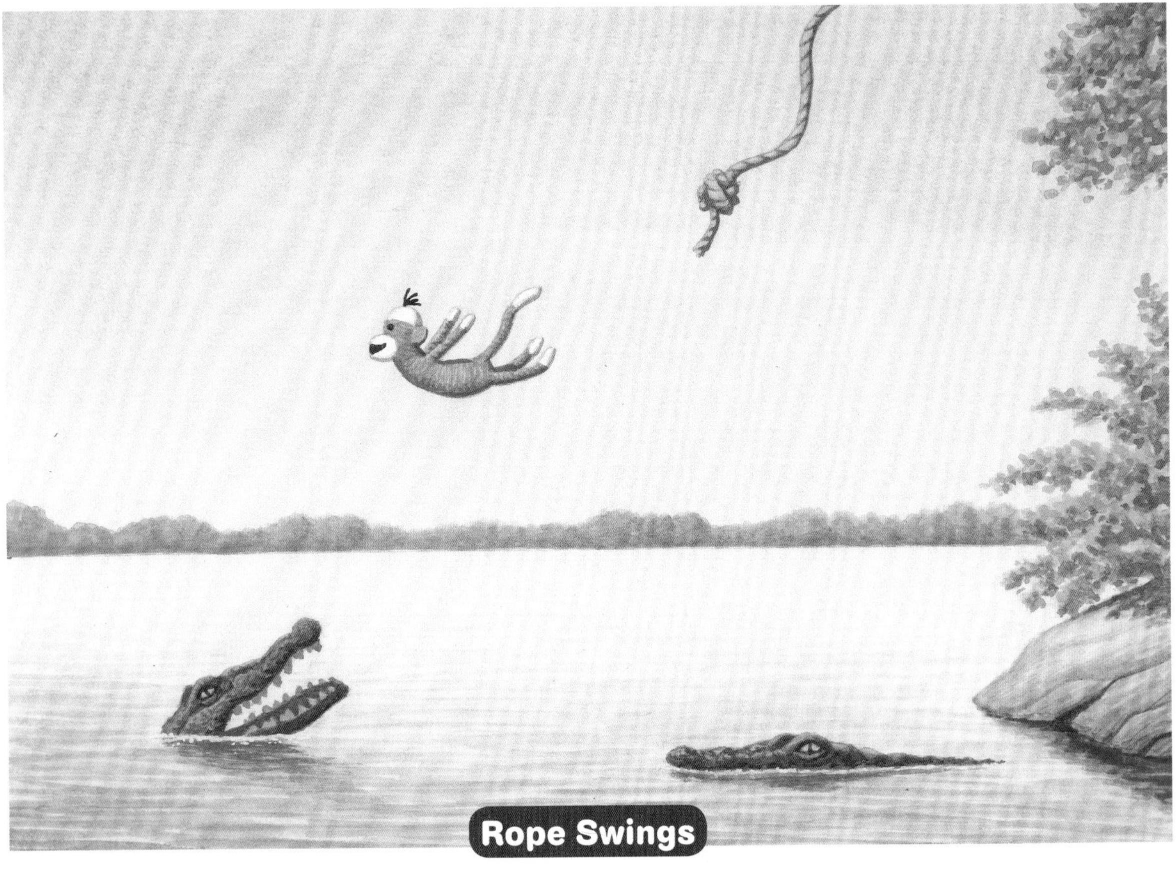
Rope Swings

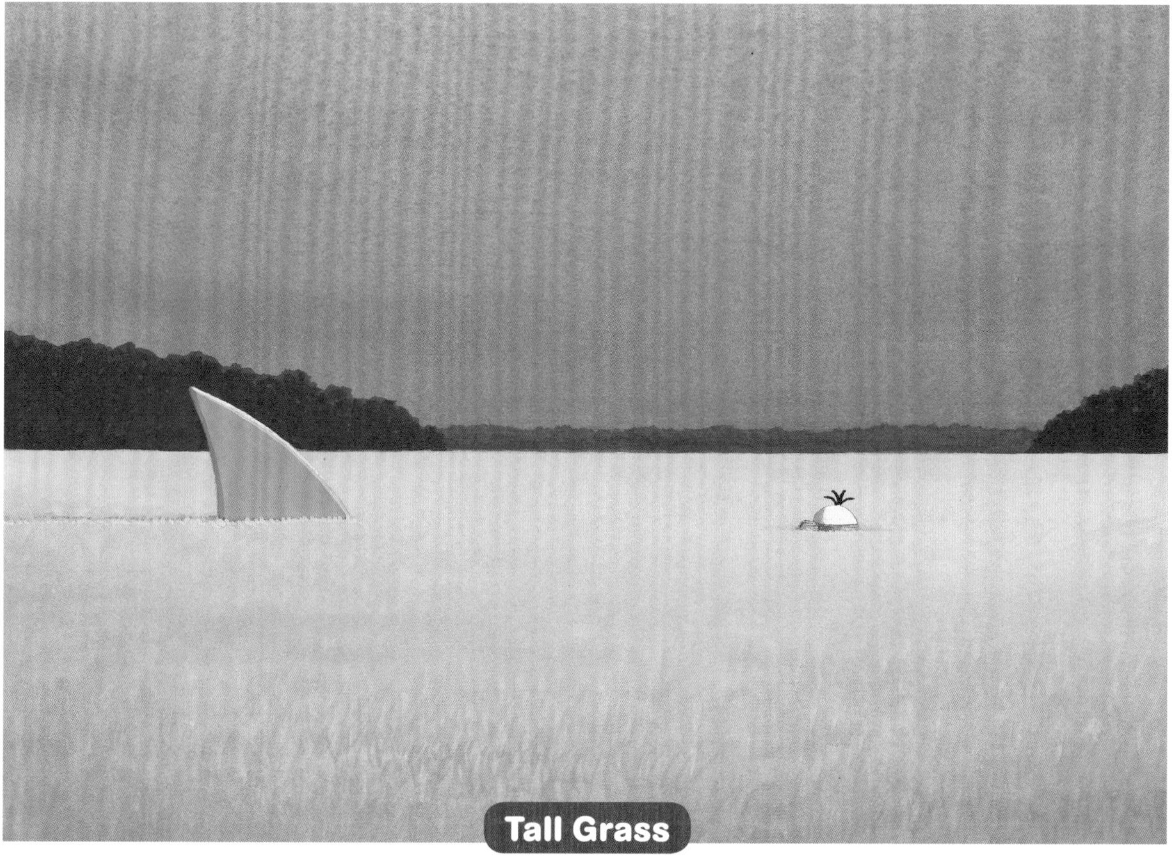
Tall Grass

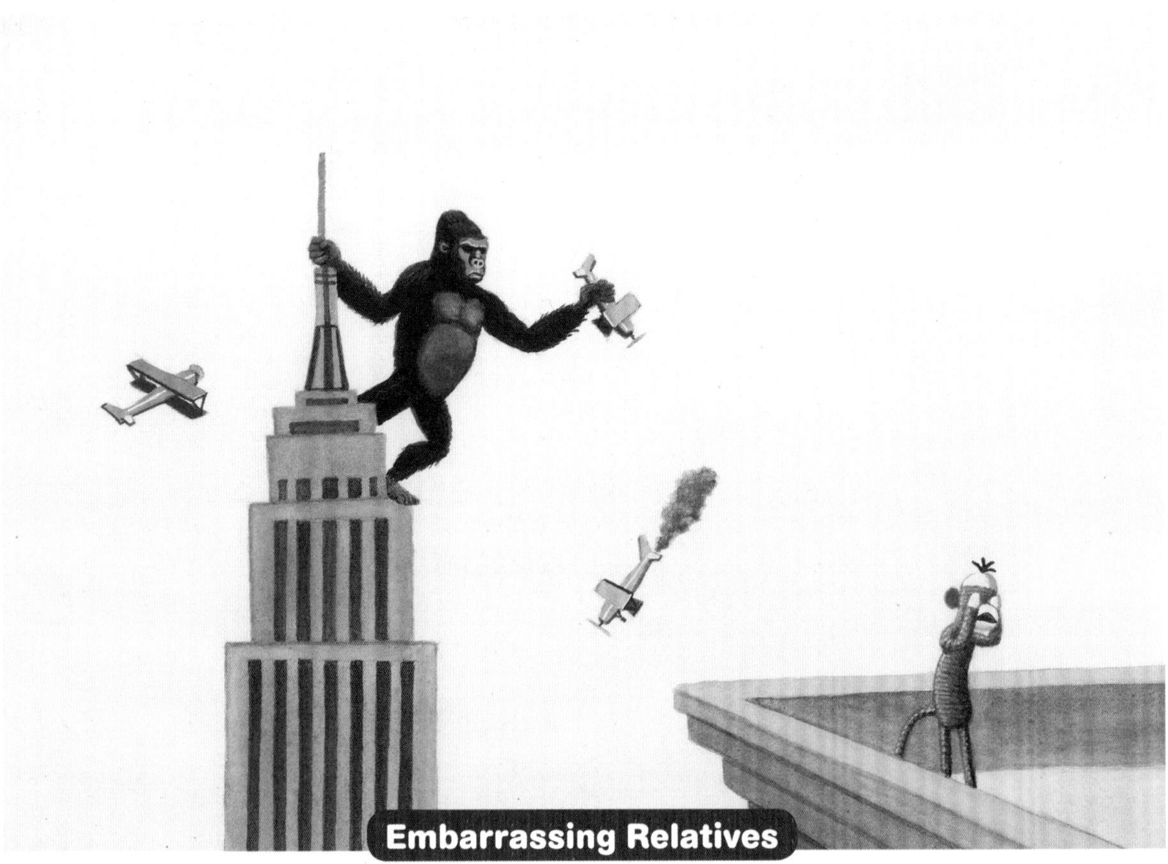

Embarrassing Relatives

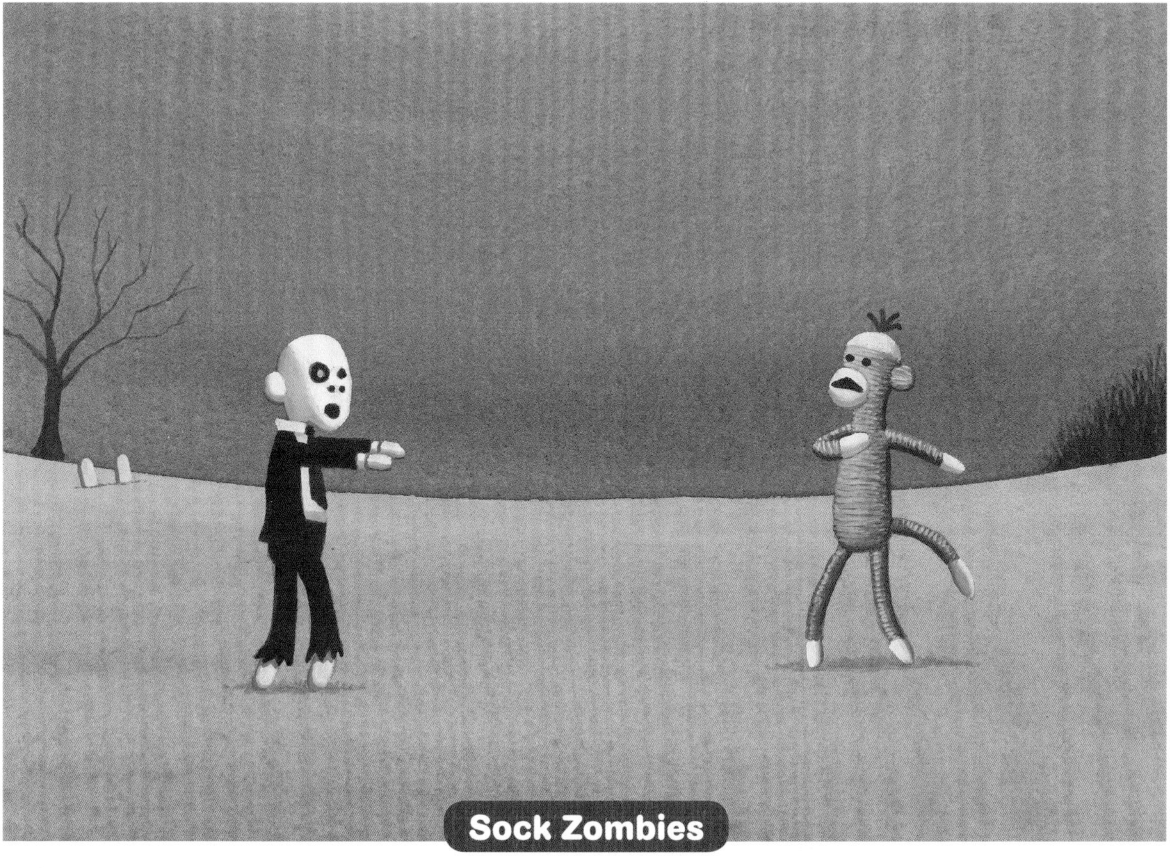

Sock Zombies

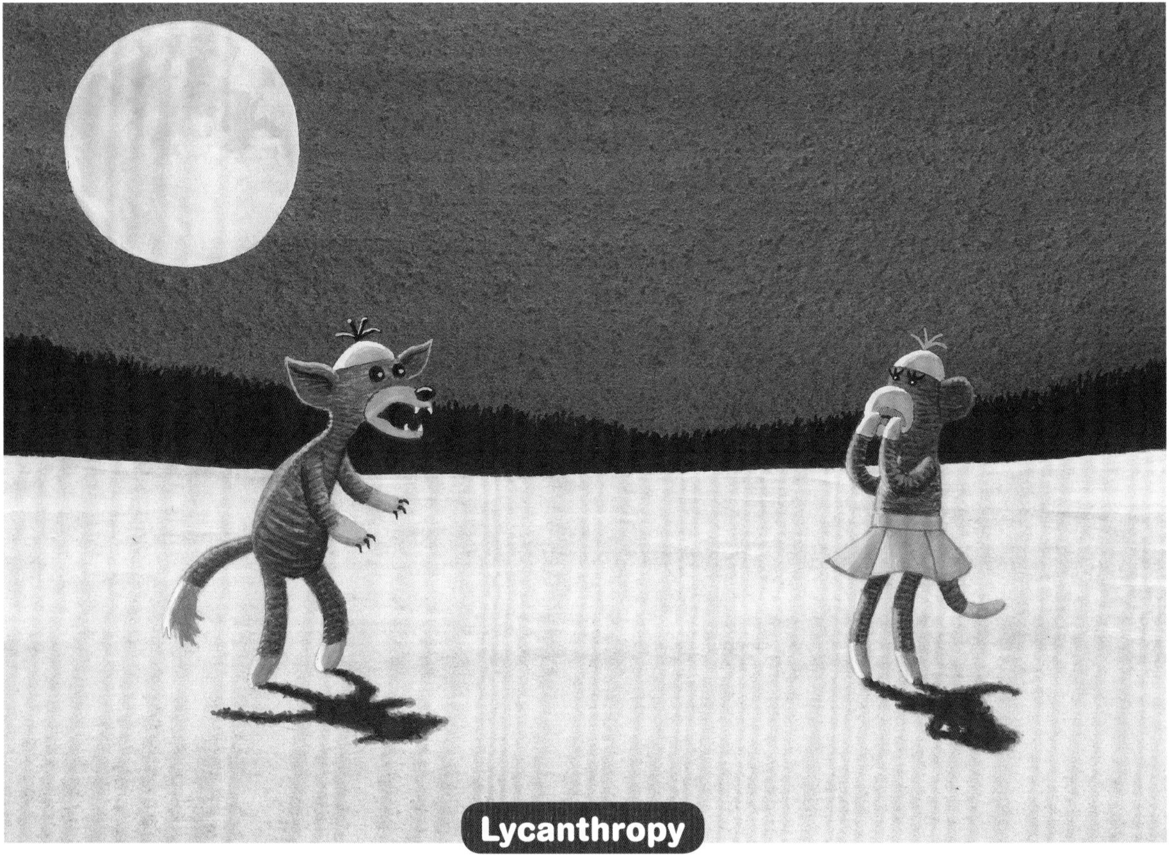
Lycanthropy

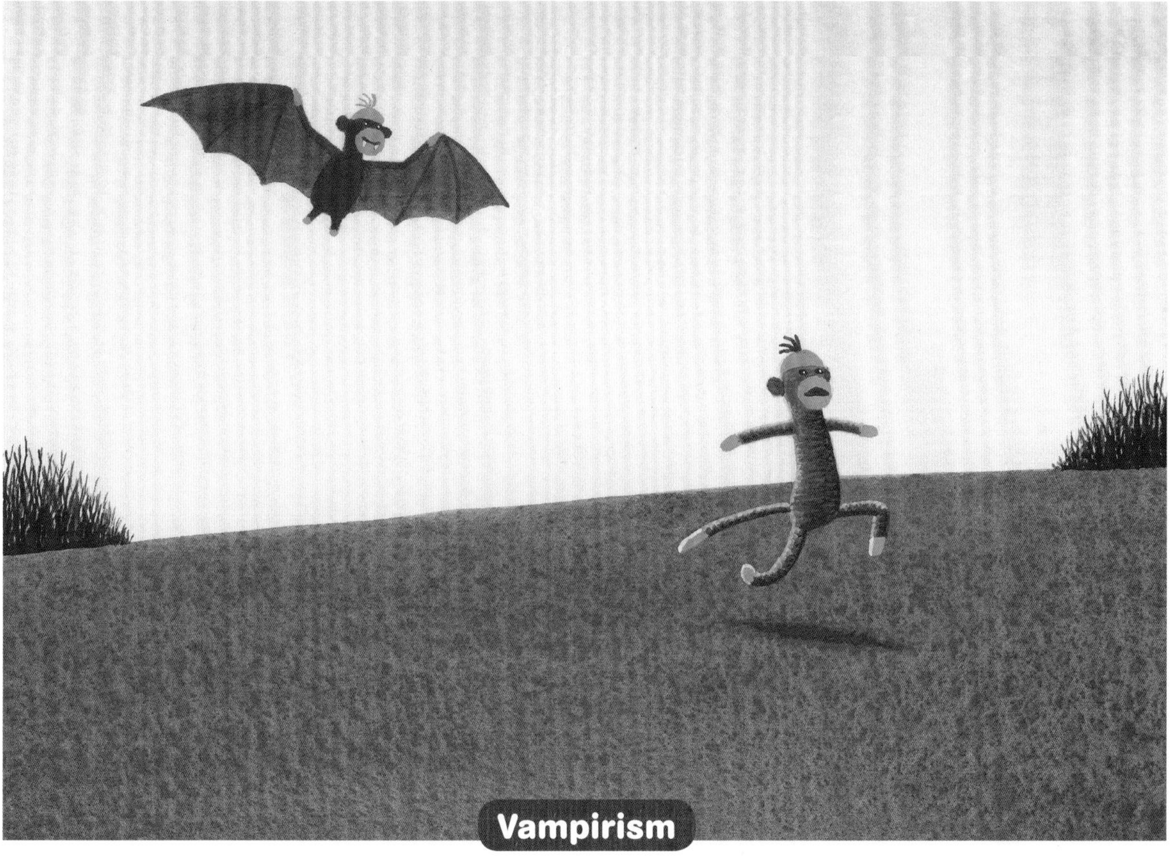
Vampirism

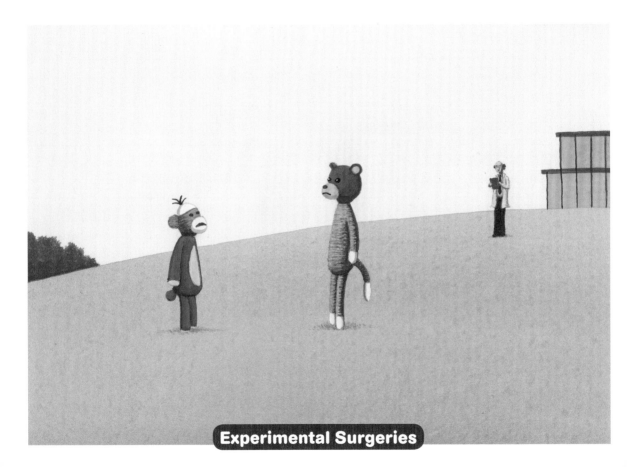

Experimental Surgeries

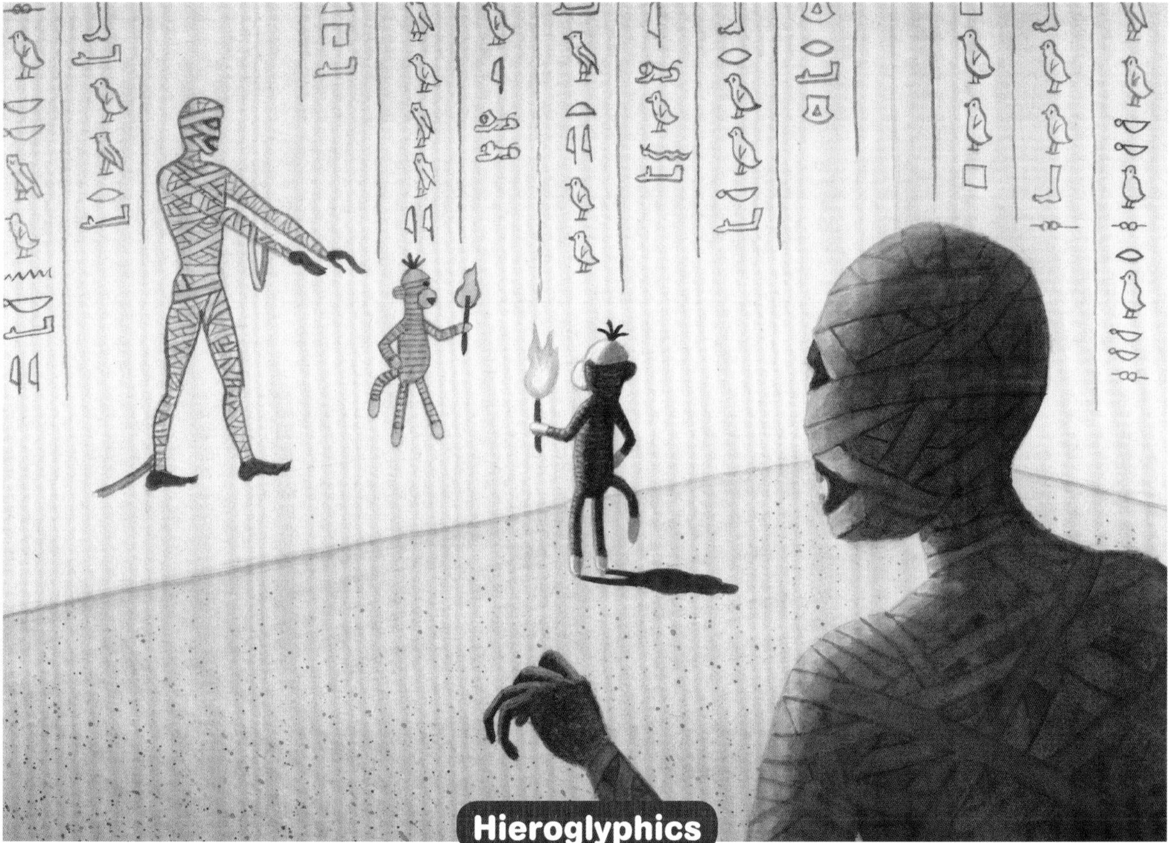

Hieroglyphics

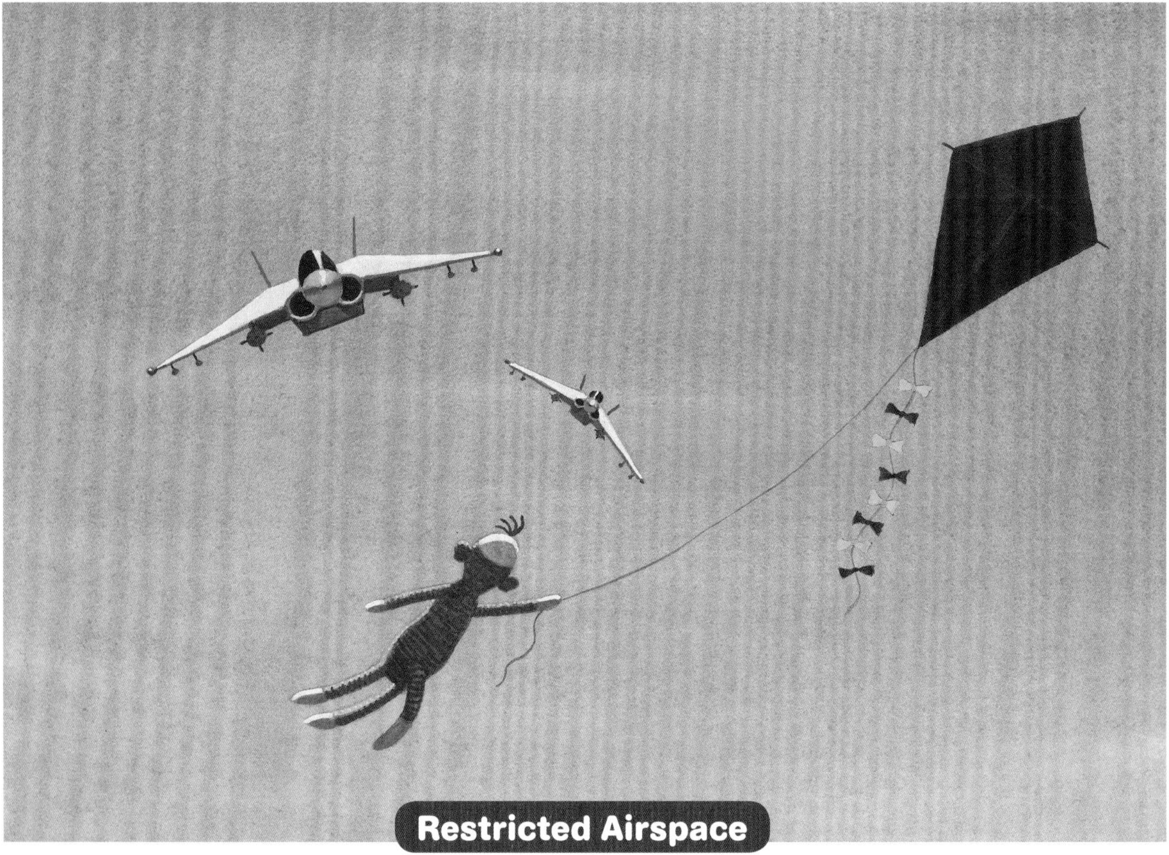

Restricted Airspace

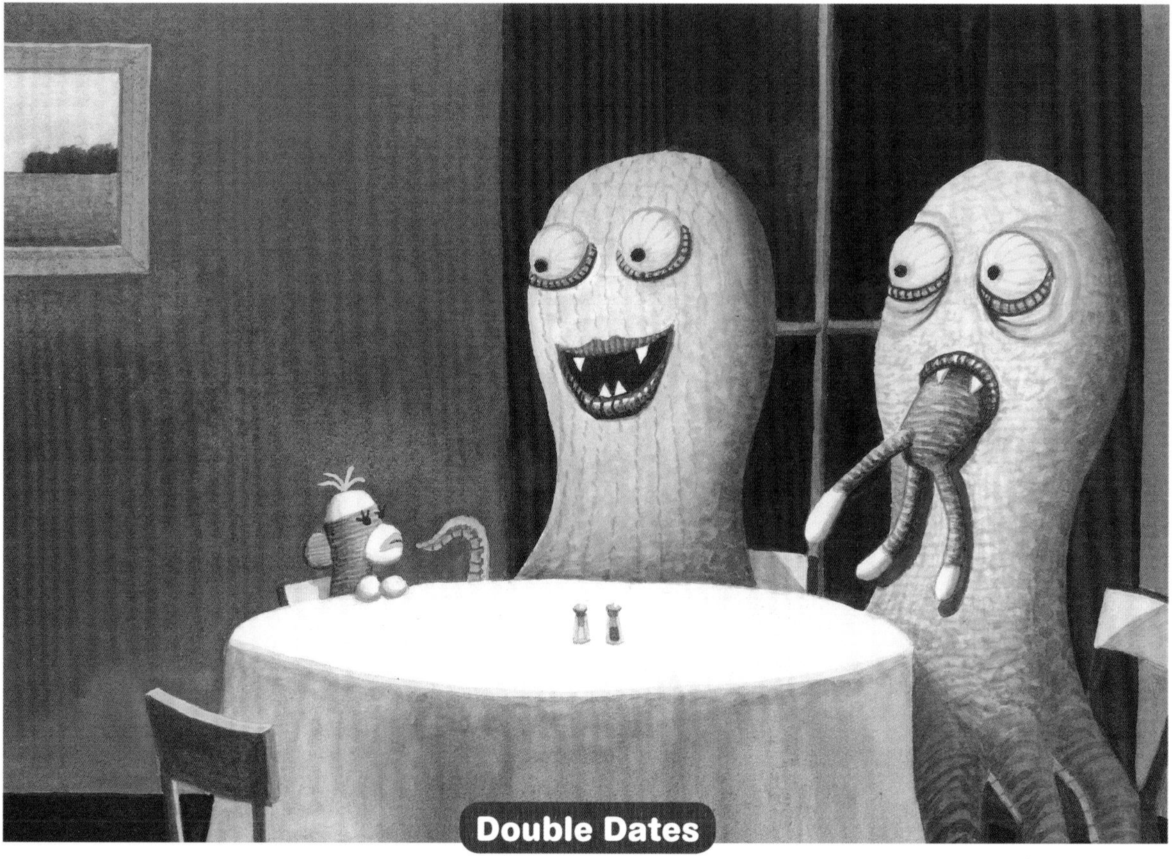

Double Dates

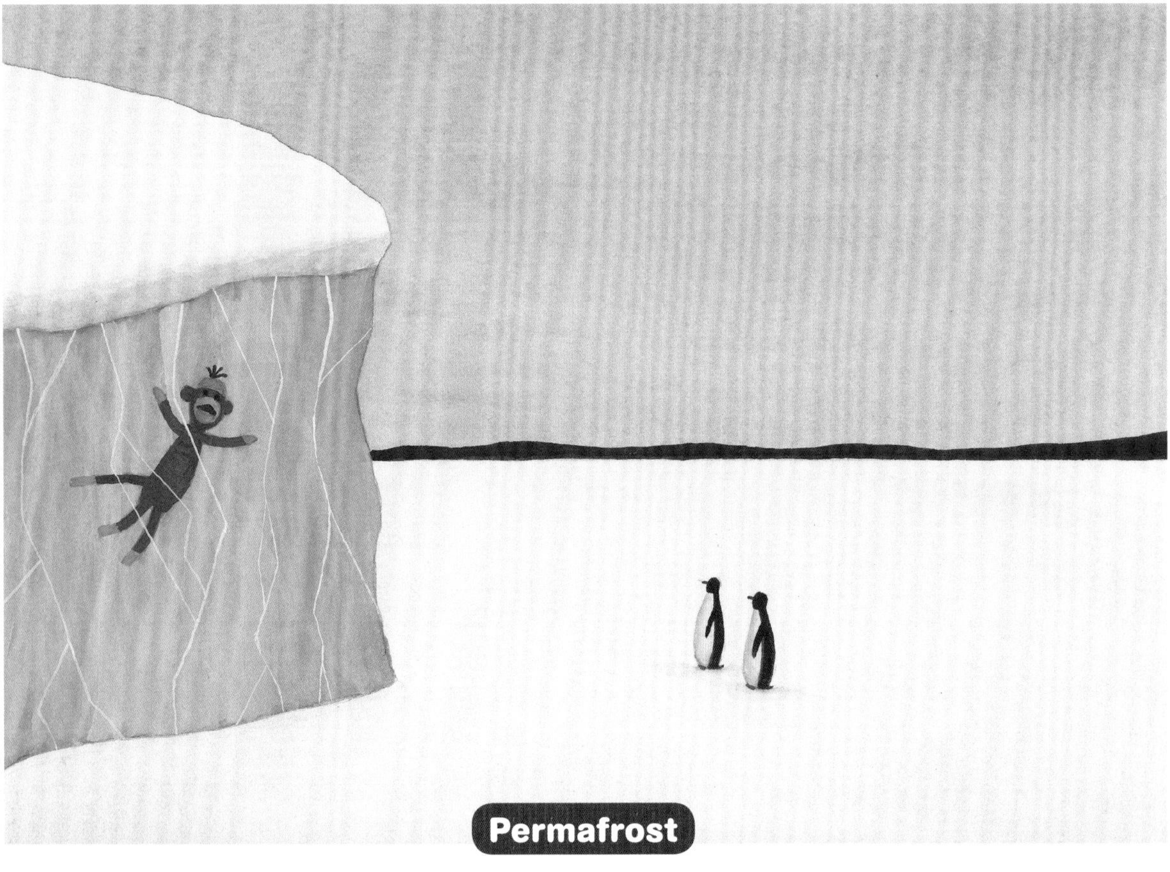
Permafrost

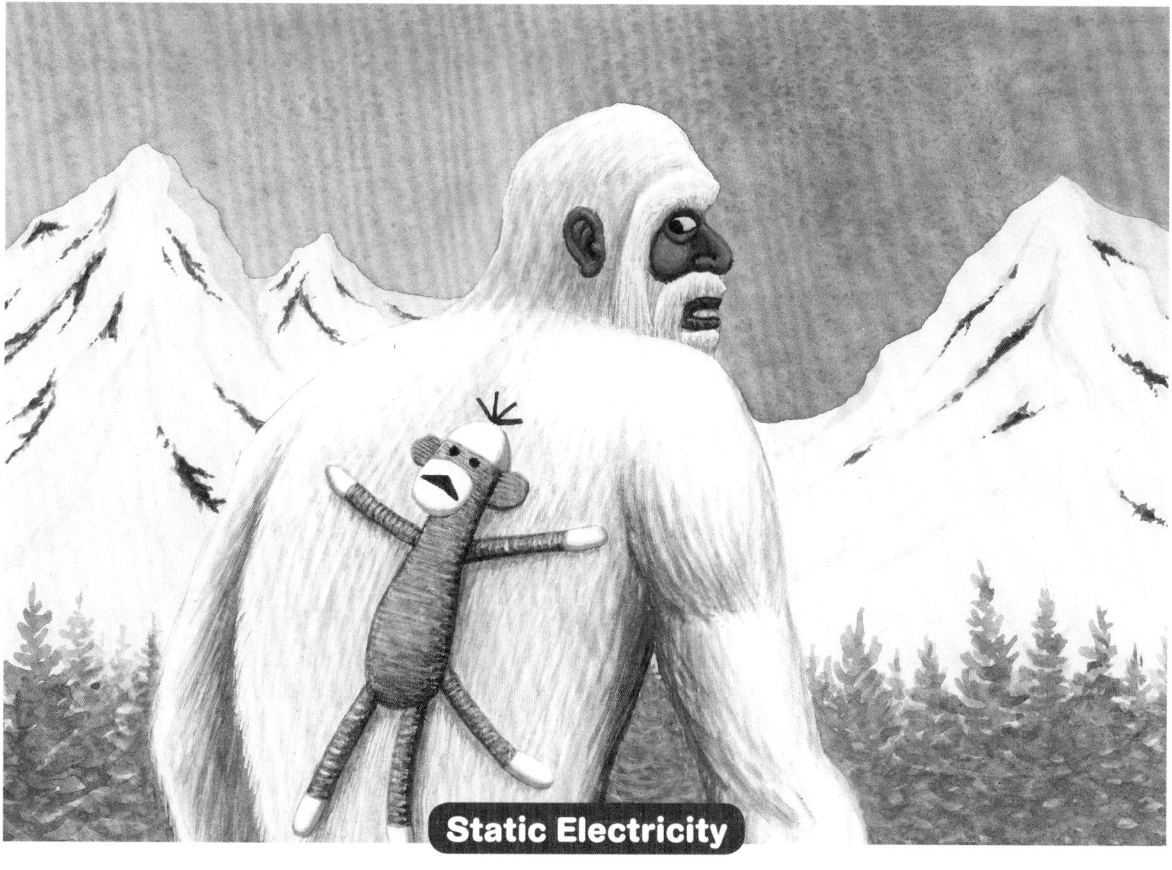
Static Electricity

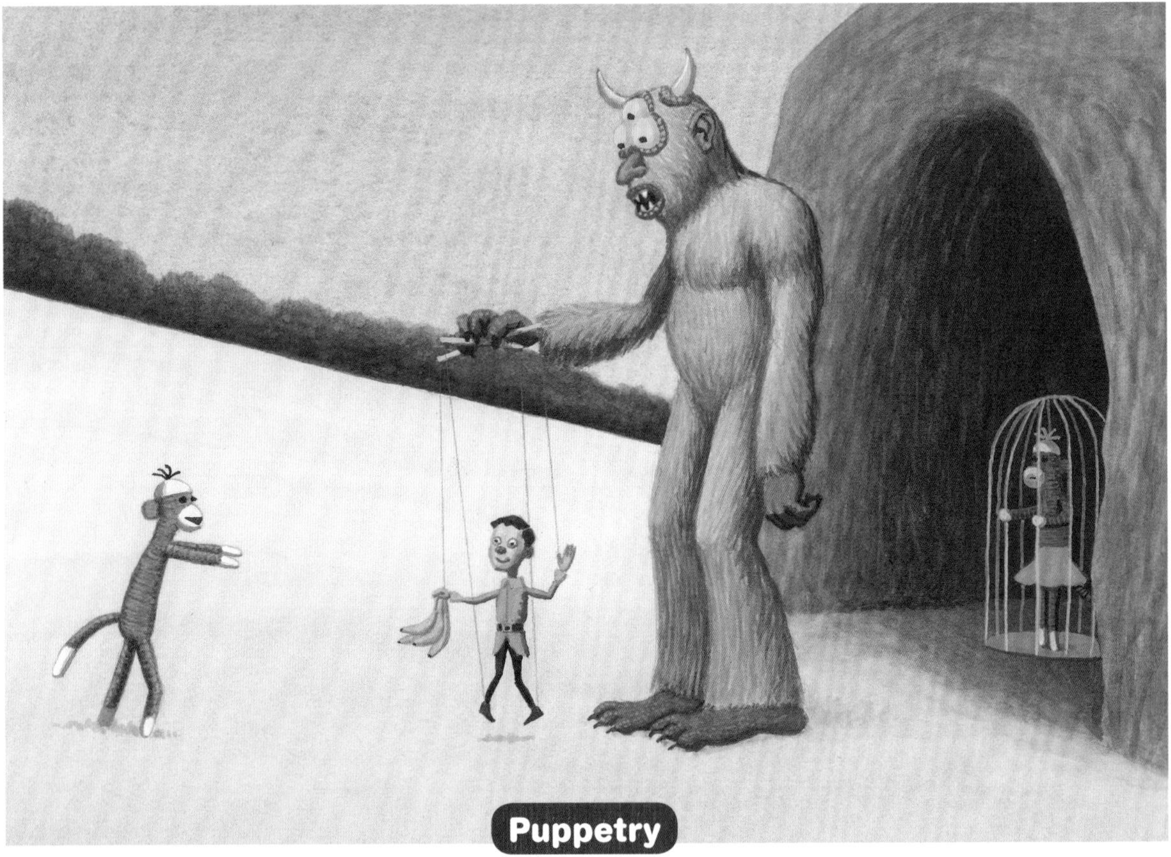

Puppetry

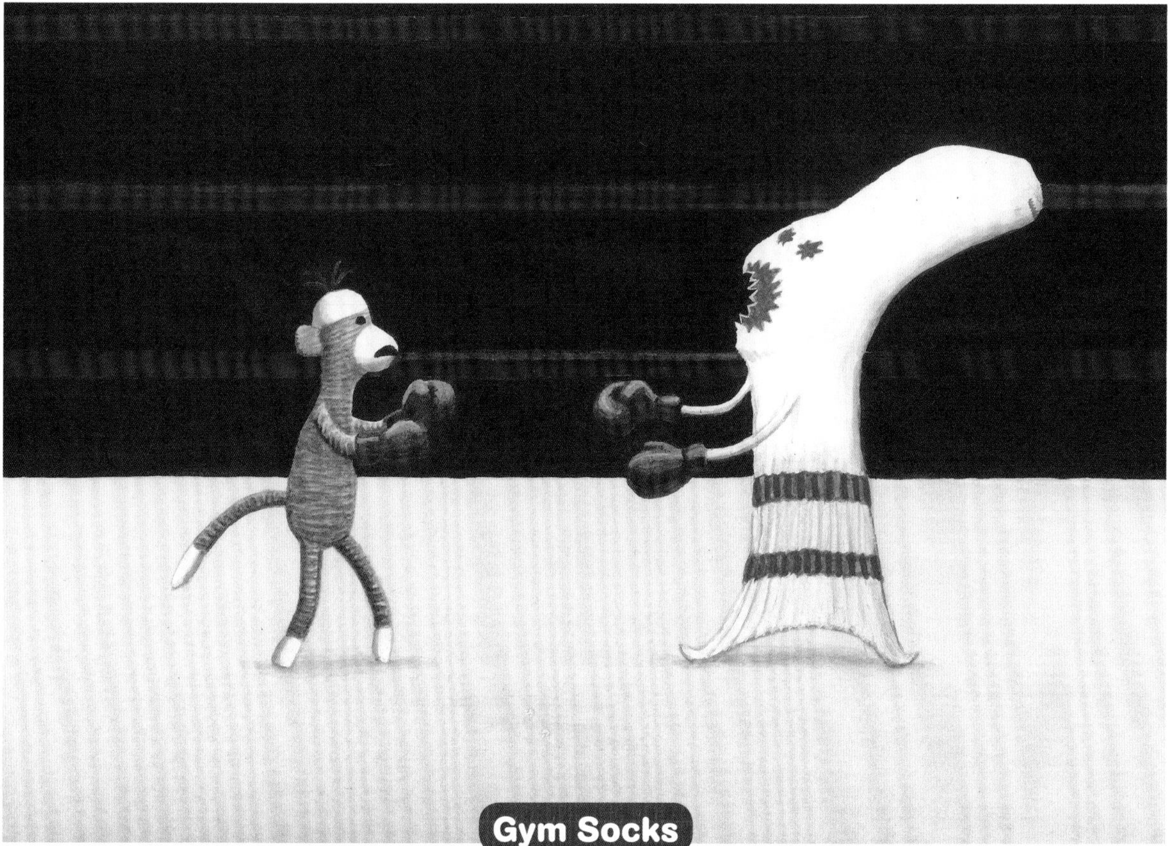

Gym Socks

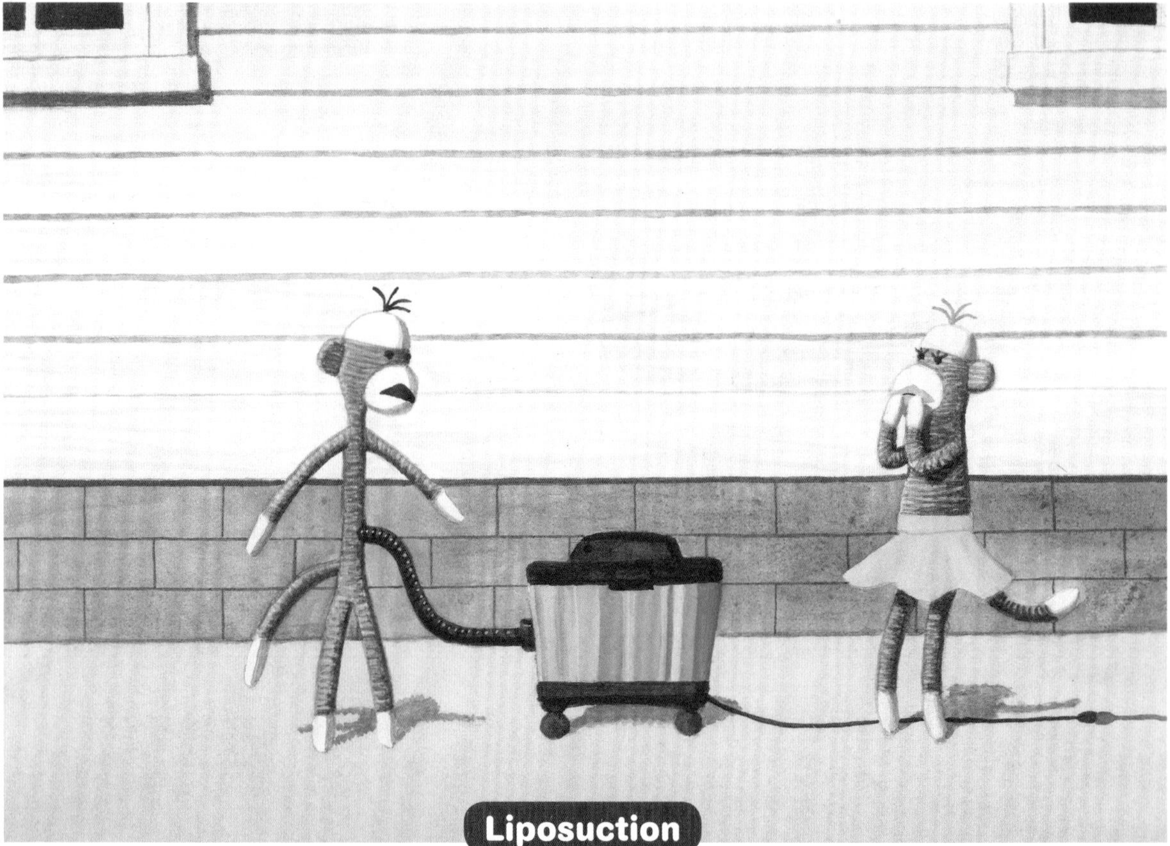

Liposuction

SOCK MONKEYS
SIMPLY ADORE . . .

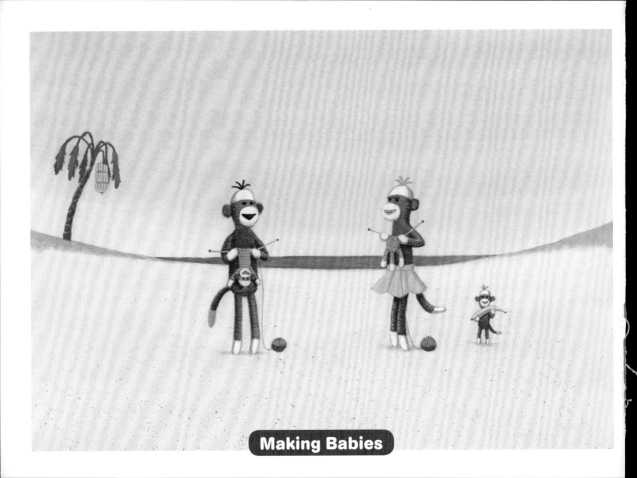

Making Babies